the
# Hiking
## Companion

the
# Hiking
# Companion

Getting the most from
the trail experience
throughout the seasons:
where to go, what to
bring, basic navigation,
and backpacking

## Michael W. Robbins

Foreword by Rick Bass

STOREY
BOOKS

*The mission of Storey Publishing is to serve our customers by publishing practical information that encourages personal independence in harmony with the environment.*

Edited by Nancy W. Ringer
Designed by Wendy Palitz and David Armario
Cover photo/illustration © Jim Gipe
Text production by Karin Stack and Jennifer Jepson Smith
Indexed by Susan Olason / Indexes & Knowledge Maps

Storey books are available for special premium and promotional uses and for customized editions. For further information, please call Storey's Custom Publishing Department at 1-800-793-9396.

Printed in the United States by Versa Press
10  9  8  7  6  5  4  3  2  1

Library of Congress Cataloging-in-Publication Data

Robbins, Michael W.
  The hiking companion / Michael W. Robbins.
    p. cm.
  Includes index.
  ISBN 1-58017-429-9
  1. Hiking. I. Title.
GV199.5 .R616 2003
796.52—dc21                                                        2002152339

# Contents

# Foreword

— 

THIS IS A BOOK FULL OF GOOD IDEAS, NOT THE LEAST OF WHICH IS THE reminder that the ancient, simple act of taking a hike is a wonderful way to readjust one's gaze in the world away from one's navel, and instead to look outward, beyond the microscopic universe of the self. Paradoxically, of course, a good hike — or ski tour or backpacking trip — is one of the most indulgent things you can do for yourself, yielding results to your physical and emotional health that simply cannot be gotten in any other way.

I like what Robbins has to say about walking or hiking where you live, and utilizing your public land, which is still — at last reporting — owned by you. The pressures to divest the public of this vast and invaluable and irreplaceable resource wax and wane with various administrations and Congresses, as does the tolerance for physical assaults on that land heritage by the various extractive interests that contribute so heavily to legislators' campaign coffers . . .

One of the great things about hiking, though, is that whenever your blood starts sludging up with such thoughts, the land itself, and the supple act of moving across its many contours, warms the blood, thins the blood, and reminds the hiker of the virtues of patience and gentility and the deeper, more elemental essential truths of awe and wonder.

This book is full of useful tips, one of the most valuable of which, in my humble opinion, is always to carry duct tape. Where I live, any device or vehicle or even article of clothing that does not possess at least one scrap of that exquisite and miraculous space-silver material is deeply suspect, clearly so new-and-just-out-of-the-box as to be completely untested, which is far riskier than to be broken-but-repaired.

In this vein, Robbins's advice about carrying (or stashing) a second set of car keys is also tremendous advice — never mind why or how I know this. I like what he has to say about maps, too; even when you're lost, they can be a comfort. I like even better what he has to say about getting lost or, more commonly, not knowing where you are. Don't panic, which always compounds initial mistakes. Instead, cut your losses, sit down, regather your energy, and think things through. If you hike with any degree of frequency, it'll happen again and again. If heeded, however, Robbins's advice will save you a lot of time on the learning curve, and perhaps more than that.

A last piece of technical advice concerning Robbins's encounter in Glacier National Park: Don't go hiking with pistol-packing cowboys. A can of red pepper spray is more effective as well as forgiving. And, of course, don't cook smelly foods in bear country and don't leave behind any scraps that a wandering-through bear could find and nibble, before making the calculation that people = food. In the West (or, increasingly, anywhere), a fed bear is a dead bear; no good can come of any relationship in which a bear associates people with food.

Notepaper and pen, matches, moleskin, hat, small flashlight, decent gloves — all good ideas for hiking, of course. But beyond the practical, be aware, too, of the seemingly magical "glide," or reverie, about which Robbins writes so eloquently, in which, after some initial roughness and weariness is ironed out, the proverbial second wind arrives, mentally as well as physically. Robbins describes this process — the flow of the imagination as it engages with a physical landscape, and the therapeutic patter of silent conversations and thoughts that occur within one's self while hiking, figuring out relationships, figuring out who said what and why, figuring out almost everything — as well as I have ever seen it addressed.

In taking care of yourself — in treating yourself to a hike — no matter what the condition of the day's weather, nor your physical state afterward, you invariably emerge better able to take care of yourself, your place in the world, and those around you. This, in particular, is one of the greatest treasures and legacies of our public lands — not the scant and puny last few board feet of timber that can be liquidated, nor the ore dug and clawed out from beneath the public's strongbox — but, far more valuable, the thing, the land itself, intact and giving us solace in troubled times. It's free, this hiking about on public land, and it's healthy and legal. It's what we were made for.

RICK BASS

# The Rewards of Hiking

—

*Ever wonder what's over the next hill?*
*Or beyond the horizon?*

Why go hiking?

At the level of just "taking a walk," motives are few and obvious: Get out of the house. Get some fresh air. Exercise. Take in a change of scenery. Most of these itches would be scratched by a walk around the block. But for many Americans, taking a walk around the block isn't as simple as it once was and ought to be. Many suburban neighborhoods are so committed to the primacy of the automobile that they are an obstacle course to strolling humans. Sidewalks are scarce, roads are narrow with blind curves, and traffic moves quickly. In such places, taking a walk is not a soothing experience but an anxious one. Walking feels dangerous. And even if the proximity to fast-moving traffic is not directly hazardous, the onslaught of noise and exhaust fumes offends the ears and pains the lungs.

In some suburban locales where the houses are attractive, the landscaping is appealing and varied, and the roads are safe but walking is not a common activity, walkers may be regarded with not-so-subtle suspicion. (Not to mention the hostile dogs barking ferociously as you pass or, even worse, venturing out for a closer examination of your ankles.) If for whatever reason you don't look like most local residents, homeowners may wonder who you are and what you're up to in their neighborhood. While out walking — in a neighborhood I once lived in — I've been stopped by policemen in radio cars for no reason other than the fact that I was walking along a residential road, and to the police officers that constituted odd and suspicious behavior.

There are much more rewarding places to be than on suburban sidewalks. Venture farther afield. Take a *hike*.

When you change your thinking from "walk" to "hike," you open yourself to a new range of experiences that this book will elaborate upon.

Hiking, to me, means getting into natural surroundings. We're talking here not of simple greenery (golf courses are green, botanic gardens are green, Astroturf is green) but of actual nature, that is, a locale where the hand of man has not relentlessly shaped every space, every surface, and every vista. Hiking also means making a commitment to a certain significant distance. You don't need to measure your mileage and consider your hike a success only if you're setting some kind of time/distance record, but you should be moving along at least for a couple of miles or a couple of hours. To me, a hike happens when you can see some different vistas and work up a sweat. The point is to give yourself a chance for an *experience* with nature.

Of course, a truth so obvious that it almost goes without saying is that hiking is good exercise. When I have not hiked or bicycled or otherwise exercised for a while (I can't claim to hike and write at the same time), I always notice that in the first 30 minutes or so on a trail I feel every muscle working, feel my breathing start changing. If it's a steep trail, I always wonder whether I'm really up to it this time. Then I walk right through that feeling, and within an hour or so I'm moving easily, whatever the type of terrain, fully warmed up. When that happens, I feel that I could hike all day.

A hike opens the door to adventure. It is a step into the unknown. Even if you are traipsing through a nearby and well-used state park, even if you are taking a familiar trail that you and your friends have traversed many times, a hike is an adventure simply because you cannot know in advance all that you will see and hear, whom you might meet, and what might happen. Of course, there are so many hiking trails within an easy drive of where most of us live that you could hike a new trail every weekend for months at a time before having to repeat a trail. And let's not forget that trails change with the seasons. A trail hiked in spring is not the same trail in early winter. The element of surprise is always with you.

Once, in the rugged high desert region of northern New Mexico, my wife and I decided to strike out across a sage flat to a nearby butte and hike to the top. It was just a whim, a matter of simple curiosity. We had our day packs filled with the essentials — including lunch for two — and we wanted to see what was on top and what the view might offer.

*butte in a vast Southwest vista*

We were then on a back road in Rio Arriba County, northwest of Espanola and probably within the boundaries of the Carson National Forest. We set off on a direct line across the flat toward what appeared to be a simple, flat-topped, red-rock formation rising up maybe 300 feet from the desert floor.

When we reached the flank of the butte and looked up, we got our first surprise. Much of it was not rock at all but, rather, a pale, crumbly, deeply furrowed substance that seemed to be an aggregate of soft sandstone, caliche (a type of calcium carbonate), and plain old dried mud. The butte was steep but not sheer and, as crumbly as it was, still readily climbable. We figured out a zigzagging route and started up, thinking that we'd reach the top in 20 minutes.

Our next surprise was that the butte was taller than we thought, and the going was far slower. It took the better part of two hours of scrambling and clambering and sending down showers of dirt and rock for us to reach the summit. Part of the problem was that we could not see from below how much the top third or so of the butte's sides sloped back and away from us. It wasn't as steep as it looked from below, but there was a lot more ground to cover. When we looked back, pausing for drinks from our water bottles, our white van parked alongside the road looked very small and very far away.

The flat summit was as distinctive in shape as a tabletop, and when we pulled up over the edge and stood up, we got another surprise. This was no isolated small butte a couple of hundred yards across, as we'd expected. It was a mesa that stretched for miles back toward a line of higher mountains to the northeast. The flat ground was grassy, even lush, with patches of trees here and there. And it rose to another level nearby, a mesa atop a mesa, that we had not seen from the road below. We walked for a while through the grass and noticed cattle grazing in the distance toward the mountains. Quite a lot of cattle. Then we noticed some buildings far off in the haze of the afternoon heat. There was a ranch on this mesa. The views in all directions, of red and orange and purple rock, buttes and other mesas, dotted with dark rabbitbrush and streaked with slickrock, were as cosmic as we'd anticipated. But the sheer size and scale of the formation we'd climbed was so different from what we had anticipated that we kept feeling as though we had clambered into one of those rhomboid rooms in a fun house where all the angles are wrong and gravity seems to pull from a wrong direction.

When we flopped down in the grass in the shadow of a cluster of scrubby pines to rest and devour our sandwiches, we were joined by three enormous black birds. Ravens. They showed an intense interest in our sandwiches and beat the air over our heads, hovering. I didn't know ravens could do that. The afternoon silence on that mesa was so complete that the loudest sound by far was the rhythmic whooshing of those ravens' wings.

Ever since that ascent to the mesa top, we have carried with us a sense that the country we are looking at from a moving car or from a hike down on the flats may be quite enticingly different from what's up top.

Surprises of another kind came my way during a much wetter hike in Maryland. Years ago, when I was active in the search for physical, on-the-ground — archeological, that is — evidence of the Colonial-era iron industry, I spent a lot of weekends exploring streams near tidewater in Maryland, Virginia, and Pennsylvania. In the eighteenth century, ironmaking, whether by means of furnaces or forges, required water-power to drive the blowing engines that kept the charcoal fuel burning at high enough temperatures to smelt iron ore. Early ironworks, therefore, were always located close to dammed or falling water and often nowhere near modern-day roads or trails. So I took to hiking upstream, *in* the streams wherever possible (but only in warm weather). I wore short hiking shorts, carried the usual pack and some dry socks, and waded the streams in old sneakers and no socks, and — predictably — I made some unpredictable finds.

At the mouth of Antietam Creek, near where it empties into the Potomac River not far above Harper's Ferry, a thriving iron business called Antietam Ironworks got underway in 1765 and a furnace on the site began supplying heavy iron cannons to the Continental forces. George Washington himself wrote a letter in 1779 underscoring the importance of renewing a contract with Antietam Ironworks for 30 eighteen-pounders. Ironmaking on lower Antietam Creek continued through the following century. But the whole works had essentially vanished by the time tropical storm Agnes hit the Northeast in June 1972, dumping up to 15 inches of rain in the Susquehanna River drainage and causing flood levels not seen in the area since 1784 and not equaled since then. Antietam was one of the creeks that was scoured by an all-time record flood.

A few weeks after Agnes had spun off into oblivion, I decided to have a look at the freshly altered banks of Antietam Creek and some of the other streams that once hosted ironworks. I got my hiking gear, including my old amphibious sneakers, plenty of insect repellent, my camera and lenses, and a strong walking stick — a must for keeping your balance on slick stream-bottom rocks and for general probing — and drove out to Washington County. The water level in the creek had fallen dramatically since the storm. While it still showed a strong flow, the creek was shallow enough that I could wade along its edges.

old stone iron-furnace stack

Quite a bit of assorted detritus had been delivered downstream by Agnes. I hiked upstream, staying close to the southeast bank where the furnace had once been located, examining the largest hunks of limestone for signs that they'd once been part of a building (iron furnaces of the time were constructed as stone stacks in the shape of a squat truncated pyramid). Eventually I came to a place where broad flat rocks lay in the streambed with only a thin sheet of water flowing over them, and I spotted what appeared to be a small human body lying in the shallow water. It was facing me and I could see its eyes, which were open. It was dressed in a dirty, sodden wrap. I froze, then made myself advance and look more closely. It was a doll, not a baby as I'd feared. Its straggly hair and round eyes were, in this setting, too lifelike. After I steadied myself, I sensed that other people might not find my disturbance credible, so I shot some photographs of the wet doll. Even in black and white, the pictures are pretty unnerving. (For the duration of my post-Agnes exploration in the region, I remained on high alert for almost any sight. Indeed, several weeks later, on a similar midstream reconnaissance in northern Maryland, I rounded a bend in near-darkness and almost stumbled over a genuine dead horse sprawled in the center of the stream. It looked to have been there since the hurricane flooding, weeks before. It was then too dark for photographs. No more hiking that evening.)

Wading upstream from the doll, I scanned the banks and examined the streambed. I noticed one unnaturally geometric shape in the muddy bank and poked at it, then began clearing around it for a better look. It was heavily rusted and tapered, clearly a piece of cast iron. I tried to pull it out of the mud bank but could not. So I dug with my stick and with my Swiss Army knife and after a time was able to drag it out. It was so heavy I dropped it in the water. Staring at the shape, I finally realized I was looking at an iron "pig" — that is to say, a crudely shaped slab of cast iron. Casts such as this were made by running out the molten iron from the furnace into a channel in the casting sand on the floor of the casting house. The channel was dug in the shape of one long line joined to a series of three-foot-long grooves that were usually made by an ironworker simply dragging the heel of his boot through the sand. This particular shape allowed the formation of iron bars that were of a convenient size and shape for sale and shipping to customers, such as blacksmiths. The overall configuration of the one line joined to the row of smaller shapes reminded ironworkers of a sow with suckling pigs — hence the general term, "pig iron."

The cast was an exciting find. It was a genuine "pig," of a type not manufactured since the time of the Civil War. I had seen a few such pigs in museums, but I'd never found one on a site. Time for photographs. And a renewed sense that you never know in advance what you're going to see on a hike.

I'm a historian, and for me, the *material* clues, the three-dimensional stuff, from the aforementioned iron pig to a rutted old stagecoach road, a gold miner's lost steam engine, a log barn, a stone bridge, a railroad right-of-way, an eighteen-pound muzzle-loading cannon, a grist mill, a lime burner, an oil well pump, an amusement park ride, or a Ford Model T — all of which I have stumbled across while hiking — are the most evocative and revealing evidence of history. Accordingly, such nonwilderness areas as Civil War battlefields, whether formal and preserved or abandoned and half-forgotten, are among my favorite places for a hike. When I can set foot upon and see the actual grounds of an important historical event, the past becomes more vivid, more convincing, more human.

South Mountain is a long forested ridge that runs north-south from Harper's Ferry, West Virginia, to the Pennsylvania border. The Appalachian Trail (AT) runs along its crest for 40 miles. This is a beautiful, accessible stretch of the AT, with views of the bucolic valleys to

*view from the eastern mountains*

the east and west. There are several state parks and natural areas along the way, all with easy hiking trails. Here the AT is more than a simple hiking trail, however. Along the slopes and passes of South Mountain in western Maryland in mid-September of 1862, a series of small bloody battles took place between Lee's Confederate army and McClellan's Union army — a prelude to the more horrific clash that would unfold just a few days later on the cornfields at nearby Antietam. When you hike here, you cross the numerous passes that were tenaciously defended by badly outnumbered Confederates under one of Lee's generals, D. H. Hill. Sharp fighting also took place at Crampton's Gap, Fox's Gap, Turner's Gap, and Boonsboro Gap, some of it at night, as Lee's men sought to hold off the Federal cavalry until the Confederates could capture Harper's Ferry and then reunite.

South Mountain is one of those battlefields that has not, under the necessity of accommodating millions of visitors, become a hushed and manicured tourist park. When you hike through these now peaceful remote passes, it takes scant imagination to look around and visualize the shooting and charges and flashes of artillery, and the shouting and dying. Union commander Major General Jesse L. Reno, who'd survived a dozen previous battles, fell here. He was just one of the 5,000 men who died on this mountain in those autumn days. An hour of hiking on these trails is far more evocative of past realities than any number of television documentaries.

One of the most appealing aspects of hiking is its open-ended potential for connecting with other interests. Birding is a prime example; if you don't mind walking along with your head tipped way back so you can squint at treetops, you're likely to see a variety of interesting birds. Most of my own observations of rare or unusual birds occurred while I was hiking. Just recently, while traversing part of the thick old second-growth forest that blankets the Taconic Range in upstate New York, my family and I flushed two barred owls, which rushed past us just overhead through the white pines. On that same day, we came upon a great blue heron nesting colony, consisting of five twiggy nests built on snags about 40 feet above the water in a swampy backwater off a dammed stream. We spotted two of the herons poised motionless in the shallow water, and while we were watching them, a third arrived by air, spread its wings, and settled onto one of the big nests. It's not unusual to see a great blue heron flying along over the treetops, with its long slender legs held straight back, but locating and observing a cluster of their nests is a rarity. On another occasion in that same area of dense woods, we heard the distinctive hammering of woodpeckers, and after circling carefully and quietly, we found that the ruckus was being made by two pileated woodpeckers. Pileated woodpeckers are not rare or endangered any more, but as the real-life prototype of Woody Woodpecker, these big, energetic, bright red-crested birds are fun to watch.

*barred owl*

Another appealing aspect of hiking for me is how automatic the work of it can become, if the direction is known, the weather is calm, and my gear is not causing any of those little niggling worries that can grow into big, attention-sucking crises, such as an uncomfortable sharp corner of the backpack that keeps poking me no matter how I readjust the contents. When all is well and everything comfortable, putting one foot in front of another seems to become a kind of lower-brain function, almost like breathing, and it frees my imagination to wander around on the landscape and among memories, ideas, and stories.

These semi-meditative occasions most often arise when I'm hiking on monotonous stretches of trail at midday, when the light seems the same for hours on end. A couple of times I've hiked along fire roads in central Montana, through second-growth forest at an unchanging altitude, and fallen into a kind of reverie in which it seemed as though I was both moving and not moving, as though I was treadmilling and the cartoonlike unchanging landscape was slowly unrolling under me. During such hikes, I've come to appreciate how truly vast the western landscape really is, to sense that I could hike at my pace for days and find no difference in where I was, how I felt, or how my surroundings looked. I have felt that same state of mind while hiking along stretches of the Appalachian Trail in Pennsylvania, where the trail follows the ridge for miles and miles atop a mountain that is fully clothed in forest. Nothing changes there for many hours.

Some people find this sort of hiking to be a bore. These monotonous intervals can be boring, especially when you're focused primarily on reaching a geographic goal, putting in the hours and miles necessary to get from a trailhead to a particular vista or campsite by a certain hour. Then hiking feels like mere transportation. But I've found these intervals to be opportunities for reflection, a kind of hike-induced waking dream. During such times, I have tried to unravel family mysteries, going over each piece of evidence, each known fact about certain relatives, and systematically tried to fit those pieces of evidence into a larger picture that makes sense and accounts for behaviors and outcomes that seemingly defy explanation. I've gone over troubled areas of relationships, playing back recent conversations, and trying to recall exactly what she said and then what I said, and then to see how what I said may have triggered what she said, and vice versa, and et cetera. I've reconstructed significant memories, pulling up and examining each remembered moment and trying to account for all the sights and sounds and smells of a larger event. I've composed songs (and, if alone, sung them). I've invented entire dramatic stories during these long, "boring" hikes, conjuring up a stageful of comic or tragic characters, describing their physical traits and personality quirks and mannerisms of speech and dress, and then set them in motion, bringing them on stage to act out a drama.

Sometimes these imaginings have led so clearly to a story that I want to preserve and work on later that I have stopped hiking and pulled out a notebook to outline the plot and characters.

Of course I don't always invent Broadway-ready drama or resolve nagging mysteries in these circumstances. But those long intervals of just hiking along allow for a kind of loose, free-ranging batting around of facts and feelings and remembrances that is otherwise difficult to find the time for during the scheduled press of a work day. Other people might dismiss such a state as the same daydreaming that accompanies other boring activities such as enduring an eternal afternoon class in economics, washing a large sinkful of dirty dishes, or mowing 10 acres of lawn with a small mower. But at some point during the hikes I love the most, whether they encompass a surprisingly charismatic mountain-scape, the dazzling light of the Cape Cod shore, the fragrant enticement of the rainforest, or thrilling mythic weather looming over an above-tree-line boulder field, I have come to place a value on those long monotonous stretches when I can put my feet on automatic pilot and turn my brain and imagination loose. That is a kind of recreation that feels like *re-creation*. Works for me. Could it work for you? There's only one way to find out.

# two

# Where to Hike

—

*This land is your land —*
*public lands and public trails*
*are everywhere*

WHEREVER POSSIBLE, DO YOUR HIKING ON PUBLIC LAND. Most states have plenty of it. The combined acreage of national parks and forests, state parks and forests, state game lands, Bureau of Land Management (BLM) lands, wildlife preserves and sanctuaries, county parks and reservations, and nonprofit local sanctuaries reaches well into the millions of acres. (Although a few states are exceptions: Texas, for one, has surprisingly little public land for its size.) And you need not head for the biggest national park to enjoy a worthy hike. Some of the first hikes I vividly remember as a child were in some county forest "reservations" in northern Ohio, where we flipped over a lot of rocks searching for newts and crayfish.

One of the advantages of hiking on public land is that most public land has been thoroughly mapped over the years. Public land also offers long-established and regularly maintained hiking trails. This makes it easy to research and select a trail to match your time/distance/interests needs. It also relieves your mind of questions about your right to be hiking there, and most questions about your safety. Woody Guthrie's famous assertion that "This land is your land" does apply to public lands, though not to every attractive property in America.

Some years ago, I was involved in research on the earliest ironmaking facilities in the original thirteen colonies. A lot of it was archival and library research, seeking technological descriptions of iron furnaces and forges and business correspondence that described what was produced and sold and in what quantities. But some of the work was field research, seeking the exact locations of eighteenth-century iron "plantations," as they were sometimes called, in Virginia, Maryland, and Pennsylvania. I found it surprising that the exact, to-the-foot locations of some fairly large (for the time) industrial installations could have been "lost" to common knowledge or even historical record. So I set out to determine not simply that Elk Forge, for instance, was "located on Elk Creek in Cecil County," but *exactly* where on Elk Creek it was located. Once I was able to find the exact location, I could make some rough determinations of the dimensions of the site and search for any aboveground remains. Usually, spending some hours pouring over descriptions, then carefully scanning the contours of the area, inch by inch on a United States Geological Survey (USGS) 7.5 minute map, was enough to narrow my search area to a couple of square miles. Then I headed out to the general location for some on-the-ground reconnaissance.

The hazards of furnace-hunting in the field included issues of trespassing. Many of the oldest iron furnaces were located on what is now private property — somebody's farm, some timber company's forest holding, a moribund industrial site, or just some absentee landowner's neglected patch of creekside woods. Hiking was often called for, because what had been a busy commercial site in the 1760s might now be a remote, roadless ravine. I always tried to secure permission to look around the land in question, simply because I know how I would feel if strangers were traipsing around on my property, even for the most innocent of reasons.

One small episode clarified the reservations I have about trespassing in search of historical truth: I sought the exact location of a furnace in what is now West Virginia — near the site in western Maryland where the first iron rails were rolled in America — and figured from my contour maps just which creek it bordered and approximately where it had to have been located. I even saw the broken dashes that indicate a dirt road leading off a county highway to what I calculated could be the site of a historically significant ironworks. So I packed up and drove to the place where the dirt road led off the highway. I found it easily and turned my go-anywhere Ford van onto a rutted, mud-slick two-track that wound down into a forest overgrown with vines. And stopped. About 50 feet in, on the right side, I saw a sign nailed to a tree. The sign itself was actually a broken-off length of weathered siding, about three feet long. On it, someone had daubed (with a stick or corn-cob but surely not with a real paintbrush), in what I hoped was merely red paint, the words "BAD DOG."

Unh-unh, I thought. I'm not putting myself down at the bottom of that particular hill — iron furnace or no iron furnace. No hiking today. Years later when I saw the film *Blair Witch Project*, I thought about that sign. It was located in the same area where the film had been shot.

Of course, hiking is possible wherever there is a rewarding setting on accessible land with good trails. Hiking in open fields or in the mountains — forested or not — brings special categories of rewards. One of the rewards that transcends any category of hiking geography is, simply, *light*. Perhaps I have spent too many hours under the yellow light of rows of bulbs or working in the blue flicker of fluorescents or the gray shimmer emanating from a Mac screen, but I have come to treasure the colors and effects of natural light in natural settings. I have been known to sit for hours watching the play of late-afternoon sunlight across a vast bare face of a mountain peak in the Rockies. "Mountain-watching," I call it, and while it may sound like watching grass grow or paint dry, it is quite a different matter. With mountain light or forest light, things *happen* and change before your eyes. Similarly, I recall a hike in a heavily forested cove deep in West

Virginia when the late light streaming through the breeze-tossed canopy of tulip trees, red oaks, and birches was so animatedly silver that my companions and I finally stopped hiking and just stretched out on a mossy bank to watch the shimmering treetops.

## FOREST HIKING

When most people think of hiking, they generally visualize a hike in the woods, and indeed most of the public lands with good hiking trails are in national parks or forests that are, well, *forests*.

To me, the very word *forest* is magical, suggesting an abundance of rich colors, shifting patterns of haunting light, textures and materials that practically ask to be touched, earthy and evocative smells, and mysterious thematic sounds. A forest changes with every step taken into it. It whispers much, but I always sense there is much more held back, much more to be discovered if I can only take the time to stop and stare and listen and sniff. And return again and again, because the forest will be different each time. Wherever I find myself in a forest, it always seems to me to be the very heart of the forest, and I feel completely surrounded by an infinite green circle of wonders to be discovered. Every vector is an opportunity.

Forests are especially rewarding sites for hiking during warm-weather months, because much of the time you'll be hiking in the shade of a complete canopy of leaves. Often, it's a little more humid in a forest than in the open field, but the sunlight is indirect and cool. Or when the weather is cool, hiking in a thickly shaded forest where sunlight is a rarity, such as in a boreal forest of pines, firs, and hemlocks, can be downright chilly and calls for a warming layer of clothing. The chorus of an old Leadbelly folk blues captures this atmosphere perfectly: "in the pines, in the pines, where the sun never shines, and the shivering cold winds blow."

Forest hiking can be especially rewarding if you are keen on spotting wildlife. I admit to being hopelessly enthusiastic about watching and listening to wild creatures of all kinds, large and small. No matter how frequently I see even the most common, and to some people even

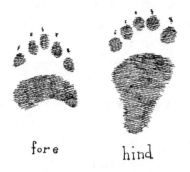

for e          hind

*bear tracks: a lucky find on a forest trail*

*annoying,* wild things, such as white-tailed deer, woodchucks, chipmunks, Canada geese, wood frogs, and garter snakes, I am always thrilled and always stop to watch them. There is a great deal of life in a forest, and any of the larger mammals that you might expect to see in North America — white-tailed deer, moose, elk, black bears, grizzly bears, mountain lions, gray wolves, foxes, beaver, porcupines, raccoons, opossums, weasels, skunks — are all forest dwellers. That's not to say you won't see some of these animals in rock or desert settings or in open fields — I once surprised a bobcat in a large fallow field in the Finger Lakes region of New York (all right, I was more surprised than the bobcat). But in general, a forest sighting is most likely.

I have encountered black bears at close range in the forests of Pennsylvania, California, New York, and Virginia. Deer, both white-tailed (in the east) and mule (in the west), have been a regular sightseeing feature in nearly every state in which I've gotten out on a trail. Once I enjoyed a long, eye-to-eye meeting with a wonderfully antlered elk on a forest trail in Yellowstone. In the same park but in another wilderness area, my photographer friend Paul Chesley, my daughter Molly, and I came around a sharp corner on a trail in deep underbrush only to find ourselves directly under the unhappy bloodshot glare of a female moose with very black fur. "Be like getting hit by a pickup truck," Paul observed as we all timidly backed up the trail in as submissive a style as we could muster. I've observed, and been observed by, beavers at work on their dams and their meals deep in a mossy second-growth forest behind the old 50-acre farm my sister once owned in western Pennsylvania, as well as in a high-altitude valley in Nevada's Ruby Mountains. I have never seen a mountain lion in the wild (though I believe more than one has seen me). My daughter Molly and I heard a mountain lion scream at dusk — not a sound you're likely ever to forget — quite near our tent camp high in the Wind River Range in western Wyoming. And hiking along damp muddy trails or lightly snowed-upon trails, I've seen the tracks of nearly every wild mammal native to North America. Fresh ones.

Both the East and the West have a surprising variety of types of forest, and it pays to know at least the basics of those types, because the hiking experience can vary in a lot of ways depending on which forest you find yourself in. Some forests are very closed in, dark, and gloomy; others are open and airy, with large trees spaced out and scant understory and comparatively long views; and still others are as thick as Hollywood jungles, with so many layers of shrubs, small trees, and vines that you can see only a few feet into the forest on either side of the trail. These different types of forests are often named for the "indicator species" or tree that's most characteristic of the whole ecosystem. Along with that type of tree (or trees) will flourish certain species of shrub, mammal, bird, reptile, insect, amphibian, and wildflower. So once you become familiar with the different types of forest, you'll have a pretty good idea of what to expect long before you step out of your car at the trailhead and look around.

## In the East, from north to south and including the Midwest, the most common types of forests include the following:

**Boreal.** The boreal forest, with its pines, spruces, and firs, is the largest, farthest north, and darkest forest in North America. It contains hard rock, bogs, blueberries, fungi in abundance, and reclusive animals considered rare anywhere else, including moose, gray wolf, wolverine, and caribou. The United States doesn't have much boreal forest, except just along the border with Canada.

**Transition.** The transition forest is, as one might suspect, a transition area between the boreal conifers and the various deciduous forests. It's more open and airy than a boreal forest, with white pines rubbing branches with sugar maples, red spruces, beeches, birches, and Eastern hemlocks. It offers more varied soils and streams, many more bird species and wildflowers, and black bear, white-tailed deer, squirrels, foxes, raccoons, weasels, and woodchucks. This type of forest covers New England, New York, Pennsylvania, and most of the upper Midwest. It was virtually all cut down and cleared by the European settlers of America and has now mostly regrown. If mature, this is a comparatively easy forest to hike in.

**Mixed Deciduous.** Now we're talking about the forests that go completely bare in the fall and leaf out in green in the spring, with a great variety of some 80 to 90 native tree species, including oak, maple, elm, hickory, beech, and ash. This is a thick forest with a lot of understory — that is, short trees like dogwood and holly and witch hazel — filling in the air beneath the canopy up top. Below the understory thrives a carpet of wildflowers, plus an abundance of amphibians, reptiles, fungi, and insects (and birds), all for the same reason: the richness of the forest floor soil. Black bear, white-tailed deer, rabbits, foxes, skunks, and raccoons make their home here. This type of forest covers much of Appalachia and the central Midwest below the Great Lakes.

**Oak and Hickory.** Oaks and hickories grow in all the deciduous forests of North America, but in the outer western limit of the eastern forests, in Arkansas and Missouri, they dominate. The oak and hickory forest is rather open, and it's a biologically rich area, so there's plenty of life on the forest floor. Uplands are dry and lowlands are wet, so the reptile populations thrive, as do the same array of mammals found in other deciduous forests to the north and east.

**Southern Hardwood.** Down along the higher reaches of the Appalachian Mountains, in a region touching western Virginia, western North Carolina, eastern Tennessee, and northern Georgia, a "crossroads" effect brings together nearly every kind of forest in the East. It's

*trail through the southern hardwood forest*

mostly deciduous at the lower elevations, but at the summits of the mountains, the spruce-fir woods is much like the boreal forest far to the north — and in between, it's everything else, with the widest range of tree species on the continent. Sugar maples, oaks, hickories, poplars, sycamores, and black locusts are common and darken the whole forest with their shade. The understory is thick, mainly with dogwood and rhododendron (which means that it's a very colorful forest in the spring). A rich forest floor, plus the vines and creepers that flourish in southern climes, make this a thick, closed-in kind of forest — a characteristic that extends to the highest elevations where the spruce and fir form a dark, shadowy, boreal-like environment. There's not much opportunity for bushwhacking in these dense woods. The mammals to be found here are the same as can be found in other deciduous forests, with perhaps more squirrels.

**Southern Pines.** On the flat sandy soils near the Atlantic coast, from southern New Jersey down through tidewater and piedmont areas and all the way in to the Deep South states along the Gulf Coast, pines predominate. Some of these southern pine forests, like the "barrens" of New Jersey, are tangled and scrubby and not much fun to hike in, but most, if mature enough, are open stands of longleaf and loblolly pine, with some oaks and little understory. These forests are easy, fragrant places to hike.

**Subtropical.** You have to travel to southern Florida to see subtropical forests. These hammocks, as they're known, are islands of dense evergreen growth in a surround of swamp, and their most prominent feature is the palm tree.

## In the West, it's harder to generalize about types of forest because the types vary as much with altitude as with the latitude. In general, from north to south, the Western types of forest are these:

**Boreal Forest.** The boreal forest ranges from coast to coast. Like the eastern boreal forest, the western boreal forest is found in the far north of the United States.

*pine tree of the boreal forest*

**Rainforest.** Temperate rainforest is rare in the United States, but it is so striking a form of forest that it's worth considering a special trip to where it's found: the Olympic peninsula in the Northwest. You'll find yourself hiking among red cedar, hemlock, and Sitka spruce that — nourished by 200 inches of rainfall a year — have towered to 300 feet or more.

**Piñon-Juniper.** Much of the drier, low-altitude areas of the West, where it is not actual desert, is carpeted by a combination of piñon and juniper. These trees are relatively short, usually growing to no more than 25 feet in height.

**California Oak-Pine.** At low elevations, much of California is chaparral (short scrub oak), oak, and pine woodland. This type of forest is usually open, dry, and hot.

**Mountain Conifers.** As elevation increases in the Sierra Nevada, the Rockies, and other western mountain ranges, evergreens of various species dominate the forests. Ponderosa pine is the most common tree, and it's usually intermixed with some oaks. As you go up, ponderosa gives way to quaking aspen in the Rockies and other ranges and to firs, western white pine, and hemlock in the Sierra Nevada. Because these areas are generally dry, with a thick evergreen canopy, there is little understory, and so this type of forest is open, parklike, and easy to hike in. In the Rockies, the next zone up from the quaking aspen is dominated by Engelmann spruce and subalpine fir, and here the forest becomes much thicker. Finally, just short of tree line, the trees get low, scrubby, gnarly-tough, and very old. Some of the bristlecone pines found here are hundreds — even thousands — of years old.

## FIELD HIKING

In an open grassland, the hiking is usually easy because you're unlikely to traverse rocky ground and you can see more of what's around you. Field hiking can also be quite beautiful. Late on a windy day, with the light slanting in on the tall grass, there is something quite magical and even nautical about pushing through the rippling waves, especially during or after midsummer, when a profusion of wildflowers blossom among the grasses.

Over the past five decades, many farms around the country have gone fallow. Although the trees are quickly encroaching upon the now unused land, a lot of open-field areas are still available for hiking. Birding is often great in these areas, with migrant waterfowl if you're near

*raven*

water or the ground-dwelling chickenlike large birds, such as grouse, quail, pheasant, and partridge, some of which have a disconcerting practice of holding very still until you are about to step on them and then noisily exploding into flight and startling the bejeezus out of you. The unmistakable wild turkey is a common sight, as are hawks soaring overhead in search of prey. There'll be other wildlife more or less under-foot, including mice, rabbits, foxes, woodchucks, bobcats, and snakes. Deer will venture out to graze in open grassland as long as they have access to nearby forest shelter. In the East, this means a post-hike check for deer ticks is necessary.

## MOUNTAIN HIKING

Mountain hiking is my favorite kind of hiking. I like the quality of the air when I get some altitude under my feet. It's clearer, drier, cooler. I don't much like humidity and I'm not fond of insects, and both seem diminished the higher I go. The long views are appealing, and it seems to me that vistas change more.

Everyone who hikes probably hikes for personal reasons. Looking out over a valley or flatland or adjacent ranges of hills and mountains or the ocean from the vantage point of a high clear peak is, to me, the best way to see the world. Many times I've found that the most rewarding time of any hike is the time I can spend at a summit, just gazing around at the sweep of miles, examining the details, watching for movement, and taking in the gradual changes of color and light as the sun shifts and the shadows lengthen. The views in the Rockies and California's Sierra Nevada are the most dramatic on the continent, in my opinion, but I am fully satisfied with the scene that spreads out in the Shenandoah Valley from outcrops of the Blue Ridge, the green slopes of Vermont as seen from Massachusett's Mount Greylock, or the sugar-cube farmhouses and quilt-neat farms of the Schuylkill Valley observed from the vantage point of Hawk Mountain in Pennsylvania's Allegheny Mountains. And as far as I'm concerned, there is no better way to see — and feel — the vast reach of the Pacific Ocean than from the summit rim of Haleakala volcano on Maui.

The play of light on the mountains is one of the most sublime aspects of being out in the natural world. Its appeal is so strong that legions of artists and photographers have devoted their lives to appreciating it. Think only of Thomas Cole and Alfred Bierstadt, and Ansel Adams, Elliot Porter, and Galen Rowell.

## DESERT HIKING

The United States is home to some serious and stunningly beautiful deserts. In terms of sun and temperature and thirst, they also can be hazardous. Hiking in the desert is something of an acquired taste. The desert *Meister* himself, Edward Abbey, was of a mixed opinion about it, proclaiming his love at first sight of a desert and counseling others to stay the hell out. "The Great American Desert is an awful place," he wrote. "People get hurt, get sick, get lost out there. Even if you survive, which is not certain, you will have a miserable time." Although it is certain that Abbey recommended not hiking in the desert because he wanted the place to himself, he also noted, "I firmly believe that one should never — I repeat *never* — go out into that formidable wasteland of cactus, heat, serpents, rock, scrub, and thorn without careful planning, thorough and cautious preparation, and complete — never mind the expense! — *complete* equipment." (Rules that Abbey himself was unlikely to follow.)

I have not spent a lot of time in the desert (I would rather be too cold than too hot), but a couple of hikes have given me just a hint of the kind of pull it had for Abbey. And I do understand why he wants us to stay away, to stay home and leave him alone in the desert. At the risk of drawing a crowd to a place where solitude is the preferred state,

*a long trail through the desert*

I will mention that I once took a long lone hike in far southeastern Utah, at a place called Hovenweep. The actual National Monument part of Hovenweep is small, less than 800 acres, and the guidebooks describe it matter-of-factly as a group of six Anasazi sites — stone ruins, that is — probably about a thousand years old. It looks and feels eternal. *Hovenweep* is the Ute term for "deserted valley," and that it is. I walked for miles among large clumps of sage, from one small cluster of stone towers to another, always mindful of the smell of sun-heated sage and the persistent wind blowing from what looked to be the ends of the earth. Photographs and a written description cannot do justice to the feeling of passing through so vast a place with that perfect blue dome of sky overhead and silent desert in every direction. All I could hear was my own scratchy noises — shoes crunching along, breath going in and out, water bottle sloshing faintly — having no impact whatsoever on this world. I thought: If Thoreau had *really* wanted to drive life into a corner, he should have come to Hovenweep.

## FINDING A TRAIL

Within the categories of public lands that offer hiking opportunities — which is nearly all of them — I like to scan guidebooks to find a place offering some special quality or attraction. If you are a goal-oriented person, a waterfall, a stand of old-growth forest, a fishing lake, or a long, long view can provide the motivation for organizing and planning a rewarding hike. There are numerous guides to the parks, forests, sanctuaries, preserves, and monuments found in each state, whether published by the state itself or by a private publisher. The best of these guides can provide a good idea of the choices for hiking. And every state in the Union has a comprehensive web site detailing the hiking opportunities of its parks, forests, and recreation areas. It's a great way to scan the full range of possibilities.

Pennsylvania, one of the wilder large states east of the Mississippi, contains one national forest and part of a national recreation area, 2 million acres of state forest, over 1 million acres of state game land, and over 120 state parks, 67 of which have designated hiking trails. Then, of course, there are 21 long-distance trails, including a 230-mile segment of the Appalachian Trail, the 141-mile Baker Trail, the 70-mile Laurel Highlands Trail, the 85-mile Susquehannock Trail, and the 30-mile West Rim Trail, which runs through some rough, remote country and leads to views of the deep Pine Creek gorge known as Pennsylvania's "Grand Canyon."

Every category of Pennsylvania's hiking opportunities, in every park, in every forest, and on virtually every trail, has some distinctive feature that makes it a possible goal or organizing principle for a memorable hike. I know of one trail that's great for birding, especially for spotting migrant raptors in the spring and autumn. Another has a magnificent stand of truly untouched old-growth hemlock forest with over 30 waterfalls. Another tours a former ironmaking plantation, with the trail leading to and around the stone foundations and remains of an eighteenth-century furnace complex. Another leads to a lake with surprisingly good pike fishing. Another follows the towpath of a nineteenth-century canal, complete with locks, dams, and restored limestone lock-keeper cottages. This is just a sampling from one populous state not exactly famous for wilderness. But you get the idea.

Among national and state parks, the most popular, best-known, and most accessible parks are likely to be the most heavily used and the most crowded on weekends. So if it's solitude you seek, and some real sense of what the land was like before all these other people began milling around, go for the lesser-known public lands that are near the most popular parks. I call these the "near-great" places, and often they can provide a superior hiking experience. Hiking trails that branch off from Skyline Drive in the Shenandoah National Park in Virginia are very inviting, but the park's 500 miles of trails are very popular with weekenders from Baltimore, Washington, and Richmond. Nearby, the George Washington National Forest, with over a million wooded acres in Virginia, offers an uncrowded alternative. Often, I've cut right through the slow-moving sightseers on the Skyline Drive to cross the Shenandoah and go hiking in the Massanutten Mountain area of the G.W. National Forest, and found no one else there. Same hardwood forests, same elevations and valley views, and hundreds of miles of trails — all to myself.

Great Smoky Mountains National Park in Tennessee is undeniably one of the great parks, with over 800 miles of trails. But it's also the most popular park in the NPS system, drawing over 10 million visitors a year. Most of them probably don't stray very far from their cars, but it's still a fairly crowded park. However, much the same kind of southern highlands hiking experience is available in the surrounding terrain known as the Cherokee National Forest in Tennessee, the Nantahala National Forest in North Carolina, and the Chattahoochee National Forest in Georgia.

Similarly, Yellowstone and Grand Teton National Parks are large and wonderful and crowded (at least along the roads, the major campsites, and lodges), but much the same classic Rocky Mountain experience — and more remote wilderness trails — can be found nearby in Wyoming's Bridger-Teton National Forest and Shoshone National Forest and in Idaho's Targhee National Forest. I have hiked in these areas on weekends in August and encountered not a single other person. Waterton-Glacier International Peace Park is a stunning scenic wilderness with more great trails than most people could hike in many seasons, but nearby in Montana's Lewis and Clark National Forest are two major wilderness areas, the Great Bear and the Bob Marshall, and they are far less popular and less congested than Glacier.

In short, when you want to hike in solitude on some great trails, look at the great places, and then look next door.

# three

# How to Hike

—

Putting one foot in front of the other
is only the beginning.

OF COURSE I KNOW HOW TO HIKE. I KNOW HOW TO WALK, after all. What's the difference?

I've heard a lot of people say this. I've said it myself. And in a general sense, it's true. But as is so often the case, it is one thing to toss off a flip remark like this while yakking with friends over lunch, and it's another thing to stick with that view when you're actually out on a trail. As is usually the case, getting out on the ground changes everything.

Some time ago, my friend Paul, a wildlife photographer, experienced mountain hiker, skier, and all-around outdoorsman, invited me to go along on a day hike in Waterton-Glacier International Peace Park (formerly known as Glacier National Park) in Montana in late August. He was keen on photographing the views from a mountaintop named Triple Divide Peak. "It's not a strenuous climb, nothing technical.

It's just about 8,000 feet high," Paul told me. He pointed out that the peak is the only place on the continent where three watersheds come together. The watershed on one side leads to the Atlantic, on another side to the Pacific, and on a third side to the Arctic Ocean.

I was skeptical of Paul's geography until I checked a map. But of course I said yes. It would be a great day hike in one of my favorite parks. Paul mentioned that we'd be hiking with a couple of other friends, summer park rangers who were off duty that day. Good hikers, he added.

One fundamental principle of enjoyable hiking is knowing the place where you're hiking and matching yourself to those conditions. So I got out my maps of Glacier, located Triple Divide Peak, then traced the trails downward toward intersections with the road and thus found the likely trailhead. Then I scaled off the distance to see how many miles we'd be hiking. As a rule of thumb, the U.S. Army's conventional marching pace is three miles per hour. It's a decent pace that anyone in good shape carrying a fair-sized pack can sustain for many hours. All day, in fact. But I also checked the contour lines to get an idea of how much of an ascent this hike might be. About 1,500 feet up from the trailhead to the ridge. A climb, but not a real "grunt." And I figured that Paul would stop frequently to shoot pictures, because it looked on the map like there was a fair amount of open land, which in Glacier means dramatic views.

I got out my well-broken-in pair of hiking boots — old Vasque/Red Wings with a lot of mileage but still some useful tread left — and a pair of shorts and a bright-colored T-shirt. I packed a lightweight pair of long cotton khaki cargo pants, a long-sleeved flannel shirt, and my bright red windbreaker — the one with a snap-on hood and big pockets that could accommodate my shortie binoculars and a small water bottle. I planned also to include in my day pack a larger water bottle, a large sandwich, several granola bars, an orange, and all the odds and ends I always carry: Swiss Army knife, a length of nylon cord, a compass, a spare pair of glasses, sunblock, and insect repellent.

I was set, I figured. Ready for anything.

On the day of the hike, Paul and I rendezvoused with the two rangers (let's call them Jesse and Doc) at their summer trailer at six o'clock in the morning. I watched Doc strap on the longest-barreled .44 magnum revolver I had ever seen outside of a Dirty Harry movie.

"Hey, what's the deal?" I asked him.

"We're going hiking in bear country," he said. "That trail to Triple Divide goes through a couple of miles of huge berry patches. It's always full of grizzlies. Especially at this time of year. We're sure to run into some of them." He shrugged. "I don't like to take chances."

He added, "Hell, if I thought there was no chance of running into any raisins (that's ranger slang for civilian hikers), I'd bring my twelve-gauge loaded with slugs. It's the only thing that'll *really* stop a griz."

Hmmm. Grizzlies. I had hiked plenty in Glacier and seen grizzlies at a distance, and their tracks and scat close up, but I always tried to plan hikes that would keep me where the bears weren't. Was I prepared to encounter a grizzly at very close range? Not really. But then, I reasoned, these guys were plenty prepared. Not because they were toting shootin' irons, but because in their workaday lives, they were actually "bear-control" rangers whose job it was to monitor the park's grizzly population. They knew it was also their job to know how the bears behave, exactly what to do when they meet one, and how to act to avoid harming themselves or the bear. Of course, the guns were merely the last-ditch option.

At the trailhead, we parked the cars and set out directly onto a clear, well-maintained forest trail. It was a cloudy humid morning, and it felt like showers could break out at any time.

The next surprise occurred within minutes. Jesse and Doc, both with their dark green uniform jackets tied around their waists, concealing their revolvers, led the way, with Paul and me following. They moved fast. *Very* fast. In fact, they were setting what promised to be a literally blistering pace. I'm in good shape and at that point had hiked in the Rockies plenty of times, but I nearly had to break into a jog to stay with them. I figured that they were just trying to hike a couple of raisins into the ground, so I kept my mouth shut and my feet moving. After a while, I checked my watch and the map and, sure enough, found that these guys were proceeding at a four-mile-per-hour pace. Uphill. I could keep up, but it was work. Until then, I hadn't realized that I could hike uphill at that pace.

Whenever we broke out of the trailside stands of Douglas fir and ponderosa and got a sweeping view of the peaks south along the Continental Divide with the cloud shadows sliding over the bare brown hide of the mountainsides, Paul stopped and got out his camera and lenses. He anticipated my question about what the hurry was and said it was a long, steep hike and he wanted to be in place on the peak when the afternoon light would be at its best. Of course. Paul was professionally determined to reach the peak at the right time, and he'd picked for hiking companions people who really knew how to cover a lot of ground. This was hiking for a purpose, not just sightseeing. These guys hiked on patrol all the time, every day all summer, on Glacier's roller-coaster trails at fairly high altitudes.

So on we went, at a pace that kept me thinking about my lungs and legs and not much else. In fact, I spent a lot of time listening to my own breathing. I generally did not have enough breath left for conversation.

*taking a break at the peak*

Jesse and Doc, by contrast, kept up a constant chatter about the trees, the berries, the bears, the colors of the rocks and what their composition might be, the quality of the water, the changes in the weather — we were showered upon a couple of times before lunch — and, of course, the latest gossip about other rangers, both male and female, and what was happening in the park that summer.

That old macho malarkey about making a strong showing and not looking like a wimp who could not cut it when the going got tough kept me, well, going when the going got tough. Competition, it seems to me, is not so much a game as an *emotion*.

When we finally stopped for lunch I was wringing wet with sweat and convinced I had lost 5 to 10 pounds since morning. My feet were buzzing from the rapid pounding they'd taken. I kept my dark thoughts about the disparities of age and condition in our party to myself. (The rangers were in their 20s. I was not.) Several things were clear. I could sustain a four-mile-per-hour marching pace if I had to, but it was not fun. I wolfed down my sandwich and could've downed at least one more. Lesson #2: If you're really going to move fast, your caloric mileage is going to suffer. Bring more food. Take more breaks. Drink more water.

And first choose your hiking companions very carefully.

When we finally reached the top, we admired the spectacular views and the geographical and philosophical implications of a triple divide. Paul got his pictures. I got the satisfaction of reaching a unique American place known to comparatively few of my fellow citizens. Then, with the sun dropping over the peaks to the west, we headed back down. Even faster. That was not a walk. That was a *hike*.

And those famous Glacier grizzlies? Never saw one, even at a distance. Not even a paw print.

Probably the most common miscalculation leading to less-than-enjoyable hiking is overestimating the ground you can cover. Three miles an hour with a light pack on fairly level terrain in favorable weather is a good rule of thumb. But change the situation to include, say, an 2,000-foot vertical climb, a rocky trail that's slippery with wet leaves or wet moss, a pair of worn or wet shoes, and seven roaring bridgeless streams to cross, and that rule-of-thumb pace becomes unattainable. If you're not accustomed to high altitudes when you undertake a strenuous high-mountain hike, your shortness of breath (if not the unpleasant symptoms of altitude sickness) will really slow you down. Because most of us spend so much time in automobiles in our daily lives, we're accustomed to thinking of a mile as a rather short unit of measure, as in "It's only five miles to the convenience store, so I'll get gas there." On the highway, five miles takes only five minutes. But when you're on foot and toting a pack, five miles of hills and a rough trail can take all day and a lot of energy to hike.

You can see and hear a lot hiking through just one mile of a mature deciduous forest, for example, or just one mile of rocky switchbacks up the face of a serious mountain. You can see and hear a lot in just 100 feet. In fact, you can see a lot of life and death in no more than a single square yard of forest floor, if you take the time to look. Edward O. Wilson, Harvard entomologist and best-selling author, once observed about a mere handful of forest-floor detritus: "This is wilderness." Unless you're participating in some kind of mad personal marathon, the distance you cover in a day hike is not something to worry about. It's far more rewarding to maximize your experience, rather than your mileage.

Accordingly, hikers who strain every nerve, muscle, and resource to hike one or more of our continental trails — the Appalachian Trail, the Continental Divide Trail, or the Pacific Crest Trail — in record time completely miss the point of hiking. Blitzing these trails at top speed makes about as much sense as running a 100-meter dash through the Metropolitan Museum or speed-reading Shakespeare's sonnets.

If for whatever reason you must reach a set distance goal in a specific number of hours, as my friend Paul often does so that he can photograph in the best light, or as you might when trying to hike along a trail from one campsite to the next known site or shelter, then calculating a pace and sticking to it makes some sense. In that case, the surest evidence of underestimating distance or overestimating your speed comes when you find yourself setting up camp after dark. I've done it many times for many reasons, and it's never been much fun.

Hiking toward a couple of days of wilderness camping above tree line in Rocky Mountain National Park, my wife and I got off to a later-than-planned start, then encountered steeper-than-anticipated trails — and we dawdled along the way, watching elk, mule deer, pikas, and yellow-bellied marmots. The result was that we were well short of our above-tree-line goal when the sun plummeted toward the horizon and clouds gathered. The light was almost gone when we established a campsite well into the dense subalpine fir forest and out of sight of the trail (as specified in our wilderness-camping permit). We prepared a romantic meal by battery lamp and candlelight, and by the time we were ready to clean up and stash food, we were in blackness so utter that we

*mule deer fawn*

could not safely move without a flashlight. When we ventured away from the campsite, of necessity, we were so concerned about not being able to find our way back that we strung up white items of clothing — which would show up starkly when we flashed our light around — in the low trees. It seemed comical, like leaving crumbs on a trail through the deep dark woods. But it worked.

Another time, some friends and I, experienced hikers all, set out for some hiking on trails in Harriman State Park, near the Hudson River in Rockland County, New York. We'd all hiked in this park before, in various seasons, and knew the general type of terrain we'd encounter, and we'd picked out a loop of trails some 3 to 4 miles long. We visualized a pleasant, not very taxing afternoon in late fall.

When we finally dragged ourselves back to our car at the trailhead not two to three hours but some six hours later, we were wet, footsore, and really tired. What went wrong? Well, we'd looked at a trail map but had not given much attention to the many trail junctions and different colors of trail blazes, and (we figured out much later) we had gotten off on a much longer, more rugged loop of trail than the one we'd planned on taking. Second, we brought along a seven-year-old boy who, as the afternoon wore on unexpectedly, ran out of patience, equanimity, and stamina and finally had to be carried. Third, it was late fall, and at that elevation we found that all the oak leaves had recently blown down and completely blanketed every inch of trail. We could easily see the course of the trail, but we could not see the many sharp-edged rocks and ankle-turning football-size boulders buried in the deep layers of brown leaves. Every step was treacherous, and we all slipped and fell down so many times that we passed through irritation to a kind of slap-happy state in which each additional pratfall was evaluated for its quality as a vaudeville *schtick*. And of course, the daylight went away before we got back to the trailhead, and had anyone thought to bring a flashlight for an "afternoon" hike? Nope. We covered more miles with more difficulty than we had ever anticipated. The upside, though, was that it was good congenial company on a gorgeous fall afternoon. So we could laugh about it. Later.

War stories aside, hiking is not always a series of mishaps. On another occasion, I did a time-and-distance calculation that worked out *exactly* as planned. It can be done. I was in Yellowstone National Park for a series of hikes, and I was interested in seeing a geyser array that was not Old Faithful, not located at the center of a population explosion. So I searched my maps for one that was well away from any pavement and parking lots and that was suitable for a day hike. The Shoshone Geyser Basin off the southwest end of Shoshone Lake seemed to fit the bill. On my contour maps it looked to be a 9- to 10-mile hike, with no more than a 500-foot elevation change over the course of the entire hike. Some ups and downs, but no slow slogs. I figured that I could cover the distance from the trailhead to the geyser basin in a maximum of four hours, spend two hours watching and looking around the geysers and fumaroles, and then take another four hours returning to the trailhead for a total of ten hours. At that time of year, the light started failing in the forest at about 6:00 P.M., and if I were to be back at my car by that time, I would need to be at the trailhead ready to hike at 8:00 A.M. This assumed a comfortable sustained pace of under three miles per hour, and no delays or mishaps, of course. The weather promised to be favorable: no storms, no rain, no lightning, only sunshine and mild temperatures. Still, I decided to factor in some extra time, so I timed my drive to the trailhead parking lot, arrived early, and actually hit the trail about 7:15 A.M.

Everything proceeded according to plan. I wore a comfortable pair of hiking boots and carried two substantial sandwiches and snacks, plus a generous supply of water and my map, camera, and notebook.

*geyser basin in Yellowstone National Park*

The trail was clear and in great shape and I was able to swing along easily, enjoying the morning light through the ponderosa and juniper stands. I watched the time and watched my pace and arrived at the first of the geysers in time for an early lunch. Then I explored the basin, looking into the deep superhot waters of the boiling springs, with their unearthly clarity and colors. The great thing was that I had the whole place to myself. Despite this being a day in late August, there was no one else around and no distracting human sounds. On the whole trek to and from the geysers, I met only three hikers, two of them through-backpackers heading north from Bechler Canyon. That's when I realized that our national parks are overcrowded only if you're behind the wheel of a car. Once you get out on a trail and put a few miles between you and the nearest parking lot, there is plenty of wildness and solitude to go around.

I shot pictures, took notes, just moseyed and looked and smelled, and then at around 2:00 p.m. started heeling and toeing back north toward Grants Pass and the Grand Loop Road. Along the way, I knew I was ahead of schedule, so I took a detour to check out Lone Star Geyser and a big field of hot springs. With all that, I still arrived at my car shortly after six. I was tired and thirsty but very happy to have gotten to the sights I sought.

On the matter of pacing yourself to go the distance, of whatever distance you're planning to go, here are some techniques to try. One thing I find myself doing is counting my steps. I feel a little sheepish about it, as it seems to approach the ultimate in witless hiking. But it's fairly automatic — I count to 100 and start over — and it's harmless and it helps me keep at least rough track of distances when I can't readily do so by consulting a map, trail markers, or landscape markers. My stride when hiking is pretty reliably four steps to cover three yards, so it's easy to calculate when I've covered a quarter mile and then a mile, and add them up. I think it's a good idea to keep some track of my pace, though not everyone shares that view and some people go hiking avowedly to escape any sense of time and schedules.

Another useful practice is to decide about how far you want to hike, and then check your map for an estimated turnaround point. In other words, figure a mileage total, then divide it in half and find that halfway point on your map. Or make the same kind of calculation for hours rather than for mileage.

Of course, like every other sensible hiker, I rest when I'm feeling tired, drink water when I'm thirsty, seek shade when I feel I've gotten enough sun, and eat a snack when I'm hungry. Hunger is simply your body's way of telling you that it's running out of fuel. But even though you attend to these basics, it's easy to lose track of yourself and your condition when you are preoccupied — perhaps talking with your hiking companion, stunned by the midday glare of the sun, or transfixed by the dawn's early light. I try to keep a rough notion of the time I'm taking and the distances I'm covering as a reminder that I should rest periodically, drink some water now and then, and eat a snack. I also pause just long enough to ask myself how I'm feeling, everywhere from head to feet. Not to sound too mechanistic about it, but checking in with yourself is a good maintenance practice and will help keep you operating smoothly without running clean out of energy, body heat, or mental focus. Especially in extreme weather or terrain conditions.

The most important asset to keep track of is your feet. Everything about hiking depends on your feet being in good condition and comfortable. Accordingly, your shoes must fit (see chapter 4) and not be the source of any chafing or binding. I believe it's a mistake to start a hike with any foot irritation, no matter how small, because foot problems do not improve under the stress of hiking. Once you have the right shoes for your hike, turn your attention to your socks. I favor thick socks, whether wool, synthetic, or a cotton blend, and I always carry a spare pair in case the pair I'm wearing get wet. When I was just approaching adolescence and starting to read and fantasize about adventures in "the North Woods" (meaning, I now realize, Canada and the Adirondacks, as the Rockies and Sierra Nevada were then not even on my geographic horizon), I chanced to read a thrilling account of a U.S. infantryman who escaped from a German prisoner-of-war camp during World War II and warily hiked for hundreds of miles through the Italian countryside — some of it very rugged — to the Allied lines and safety. I was quite struck by the attention he gave to his feet in his account, noting that he kept his shoes and socks very clean, washing and drying the socks whenever possible, and often checking the condition of his feet. He felt that keeping his feet in good shape saved his life. I filed away that information and never forgot it.

# four

# Essentials

—

Picture yourself on a
high country trail. Now
picture the weather.

EVERY BOOK ON THE OUTDOORS SEEMS TO INCLUDE A
"gear" chapter. What should I wear and what should I carry?
And how much do I have to spend? These are the usual questions. But this chapter is called "essentials" and not "hardware" or "gear" because it deals with essential preparation
before a hike and essential matters during a hike. As far as
I'm concerned, the essential *thinking* that takes place before
and during a hike is far more important than any item you
may tote or wear.

Some preliminary planning before you ever step foot out
your door for a day hike, will ensure that you enjoy a safe and
rewarding time. That's not to say it is necessary to spend hours
with maps and books, sorting your gear, developing your
checklists, and imagining a whole roster of worst-case sce-
narios. I don't believe that is necessary. But before hiking, take

these essential steps: Make a simple plan, familiarize yourself with the surrounding terrain, check on weather conditions, wear appropriate clothing, and pack intelligently.

## PLANNING YOUR HIKE

Much of your hike planning depends on your goal. Are you going out to see a particular place or thing? Do you just want to see what's over the next ridge? Are you getting out of the house for a couple of hours to stretch your legs and think things over? Maybe you just want to keep the kids occupied for a couple of hours and introduce them to a few facts of life, like falling leaves, poison ivy, muddy trails, getting thirsty, and why it's a good idea to know which way is north.

But on the balance, if you're going out for a simple one-afternoon adventure, there are a few rules of thumb that may help make the day more enjoyable: Think backward, that is to say, visualize your return at the other end of your hike. You'll be tired, warmer or colder, and thirsty. Do you really want to be hiking for two hours facing the blinding sun? Would you rather spend the time in the lowland shade or head for the high ground? All other things being equal, it is a far, far better thing to hike uphill first and hike downhill on your return. Yes, steep downhill hiking is tough on your knees. But steep uphill hiking at the end of the day when you've already burned up a ton of calories is much tougher on everything.

Try to find a loop trail of a comfortable length. State parks and other recreationally oriented public lands have plenty of these. But I would not turn away from a hike that involved going out a certain distance and then returning on the same trail. Even if your attention span is microscopic, resist the temptation to hike out a ways and then bushwhack back on an imagined "shortcut." Most woods are tricky places to navigate once you are off a trail and out of sight of a trail. Masses of trees, rocky hillsides, and thick patches of understory all have a surprising propensity to look just like other trees, hillsides, and understory. Indigenous peoples in many wild lands have developed the ability to read individual trees, boulders, and patches of moss they've seen before and remember. But since we are all far more used to navigating in a world of storefronts, street signs, and hallways, we are not the bearers of those admirable natural-world skills. Shortcuts can often turn into something far less convenient. Besides, the upside of the woods looking the same and different at the same time is that trails look surprisingly different when you follow them back the way you came in. You're going the other way, the light hits everything from an opposite angle, and, to paraphrase T. S. Eliot, you'll know the place for the first time.* I don't remember ever getting bored following the same trail back to my starting point.

## LOOK AT THE BIG PICTURE

Figuring out where you're going to be, on both a large and small scale, can help with navigation. Find your proposed hiking area on a state road map, noting the access routes and the general surroundings. Start with the obvious, noting that you'll be hiking in, for example, Colorado, in Dolores County, in a part of the San Juan Mountains north of Durango called the Weminuche Wilderness. And you'll get there by following U.S. Route 550 north to a trailhead that's located on the south side of 550 between County Road 591 and Molas Pass.

Okay so far, but you also ought to check the big picture on a topographical map so you get a clear sense of the physical lay of the land, not just the routes. Say your plan is to hike up a trail past Andrews Lake to Crater Lake, situated at the head of a valley in the West Needle Mountains (a small range of the San Juans). It looks as though the hike will be about four miles each way. You'll be in the mountains, so you need to know how high those mountains are (some are over 13,000 feet), how much elevation change you're facing (maybe 1,000 feet), and whether you'll be in forest, in open land, or even above tree line. Altitude becomes an important factor for most people at anything over 5,000 feet above

---

*That's from an apropos stanza of Eliot's *Little Gidding*: "We shall not cease from exploration/And the end of all our exploring/Will be to arrive where we started/And know the place for the first time." I recommend Eliot for reading on the trail. He often wrote about, among other topics, journeys, exploration, and remote scenery.

sea level, especially if you have not been in the mountains for a while and are accustomed to sea-level air and atmospheric pressure. I start getting severe headaches at about 7,500 feet unless I've been in the mountains near that level for a week or so. Altitude sickness is no joke. It is at least painful and disorienting, and it can have worse consequences.

On your maps, look around the area where you will be hiking. Even though you'll be carrying a good map or two (won't you?), visualize the terrain and features on all four sides of the trail you'll hike. How far would you have to hike to the west, south, east, or north to reach a road if you had to? Hiking west from the trail, it looks possible to reach Route 591 and Lime Creek, but it looks like a hell of a rugged descent. Heading south appears to be out of the question, given the many miles of 12,000- and 13,000-foot peaks, with deep ravines, you'd have to traverse before you'd reach the Animas River, and even then it's another

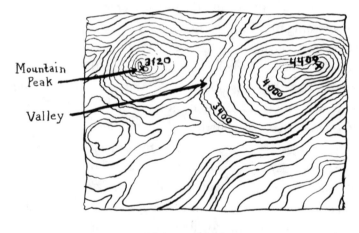

*a topographical map*

five miles or so to a dirt road. To the east, it's a comparatively short distance as the crow flies (hardly necessary to point out that hikers are not crows) to the nearest point of civilization, which happens to be the tracks of the Durango and Silverton narrow-gauge railroad, but an impressive combination of high peaks and sudden descents will stand between you and there. To the north, well, that's the way you came in. So, for all intents and purposes, you're hiking into a box. The trail leading in is also the best way to get back out. That's a smart fact to know in case of an emergency.

While sizing up the surroundings, take note of the contour interval on your map. When those wavy brown contour lines are closely spaced, they clearly indicate a lot of elevation change and tough country. But on some maps, the contour interval is not 10 feet or 20 feet but 80 feet. That's impressively steep.

These types of observations are worthwhile for any hike, whether in wilderness or not. They help you put limits, in advance, on just how far you can get lost. I always do this kind of read of the hiking area, whether it's in the San Juans or back east in the Taconic Range.

After you have done this locating and thinking about where in the world you will be, write a note describing where you intend to hike and when you plan to return, and leave it with someone who's staying home. Just in case.


## THE WEATHER

Check the weather. I know this is common sense, and I know weather can change very fast — and very dramatically at high elevations in some months. I know this because I vividly recall getting snowed upon in the Rocky Mountains in mid-August on a day when the sun had been hot and the temperature near 80 degrees when we started our day hike. Knowing the possible extremes in mountains like these, I would not only bring an extra layer or two for warmth (a fleece pullover, for example) and a windbreaker/rain jacket and hat, but would probably take along something extra in the way of protection, like a space blanket, extra socks, and even gloves. If thunderstorms are forecast for a high mountain area, stay home and hike another day.

About lightning. Once when a friend and I were hiking a wilderness trail from Cascade Falls to Andrews Pass on the west side of Rocky Mountain National Park and the weather began to close in, we encountered a Park Service wilderness ranger patrolling the trail on horseback. "What do you do in case of lightning?" we asked.

"I pray a lot," came a quick terse reply. "I ride along and pray." Seriously, he went on, when you see lightning approaching or hear thunder, get the hell below tree line as fast as you can and stay in a thick grove of trees.

Okay, but what if you're caught too far from tree line to get down to safety in a forest?

"Lie down in the lowest place you can find — that'll probably be in the trail — and wait it out."

## WHAT TO WEAR

Okay, now for the gear.

Wear bright colors. It doesn't matter whether you don a sweater, an anorak, a poncho, a windbreaker, a down vest, or a flannel shirt; bright colors are essential. And that means *color,* not white. White stands out on a city street or on a golf course, but not in the shifting light and shadow of a rocky mountainside or on the floor of a desert canyon in the sun. The point is, like a prom queen or a drag queen, you want to be seen. Camouflage-style clothes are good for urban teenagers, deer-stalkers, and Special Forces. In everyday life, I favor earth tones in apparel, but I have been wearing a bright red Gore-Tex windbreaker for years whenever I go outdoors. When it finally wears out, I will replace it with a bright orange or bright yellow jacket.

Here's why: National Geographic once sent photographer Joe Bailey and me out to capture the pictures and words for a chapter in their book *America's Majestic Canyons.* We drew one of the most majestic canyons of all — Yosemite. We spent weeks hiking the side trails from the main canyon, getting to the spectacular waterfalls and overlooks, and interviewing mountain climbers, rangers, visitors, and area residents. We camped in the major and minor campgrounds, took rock-climbing lessons, and interviewed Ansel Adams, and we even spent a couple of days hiking down into Hetch Hetchy Gorge, the Yosemite-twin canyon that was dammed and partially flooded to provide a water supply for San Francisco. We found the downriver unflooded portions of Hetch Hetchy very still, very hot, and very lonely (no one ever seems to hike there), except for the rattlesnakes and black bear family we encountered — all of them probably surprised to see any hikers.

We had finished most of our work in Yosemite when Joe learned of a vantage point in a side canyon from which late afternoon light would likely be spectacular across the top of Yosemite Valley and especially on Half Dome. It looked to be a long, steep climb, but doable in a day if we started early and the weather held. So, with very light packs, plenty of water, and lunch and snacks, off we went in the dim cool light of an early morning. We started in deep canyon shade and climbed toward the full light of day on a narrow but clean and crisply maintained trail. The trail soon assumed a configuration it would sustain all day: *switchbacks*. We were on a steep canyon face, and the trail builders had realized that the only way to walk up it was to traverse back and forth. Altitude was a wearying factor (the floor of Yosemite Valley is about 4,000 feet above sea level). I had the years and Joe had the heavy camera gear, so we were a good match in the panting-for-breath and calling-for-a-break departments. I counted the switchbacks and was dismayed when I reached 100 of them with the summit still somewhere out of sight far over our heads. At 200 switchbacks, I quit counting, figuring that no one would believe me anyway.

Joe and I never reached the summit. We had paused for a snack and a good slug of water at around 2:00 P.M., guessing we were at least three-quarters of the way to the top. Then we heard a voice. We stopped chewing and looked at each other, listening. "Did you hear that?" we both asked. The sound had been very faint, and until I strained to hear it, I had not noticed that a strong and irregular breeze was blowing up the canyon. Afternoon shadows had already pooled up at the bottom, far below us. There it was again. Someone shouting. Sounded like a young male voice, someone in distress. Sounded like "Help!" Aroused and alarmed, we stood cupping our ears and scanning like radar antennae, trying to figure out where the sound was coming from. A prank? Kids fooling around down in the campgrounds on the valley floor? A climber in real trouble? A hiker down? Minutes would pass when we could hear nothing. But eventually, we heard the voice enough times to sense that it was coming from on the canyon wall opposite us, somewhere, perhaps a couple of hundred feet, below our level. In those intervals when the wind died, it sure sounded like "Help!"

I got out my binoculars and Joe mounted his longest telephoto lens and we flattened out and braced on the warm rocks and began a systematic scanning of that canyon face. It was not a sheer wall but a steep slope like the one we'd climbed, but it had no clear-cut trail visible. There were many stunted ponderosa pines, Douglas firs, and junipers shaking and tossing in the wind, many pale boulders shining in the afternoon sun, and many deep shadows under the low trees and alongside the rocks. Many times we thought we might be looking at a leg or a torso or a waving arm and stared until our eyes watered, but it was impossible to be certain. We soon realized we were searching for a spot of color, a blue or red or purple or pink or yellow shirt or jacket. We also came to understand that if the hiker in trouble were wearing khaki shorts and a pale T-shirt — as Joe and I were — he or she would be impossible to pick out among the granite boulders and piney shadows across the way.

Eventually we decided that we simply could not locate the source of the voice and that, even if we could, some other actions would have to be taken. We agreed that Joe would leave his camera gear with me and hike at top speed down the 200+ switchbacks to the nearest trailhead/parking lot telephone (this was in the days before cell phones were common) and alert the park rangers. Joe blitzed off down the trail, and I continued to listen and scan the sunlight and shadow across the way for another 90 minutes or so, until I heard the shuddering "thump-thump-thump" of a helicopter. The scale of Yosemite is deceptive, and when the Vietnam-era olive-colored Huey beat into view, it was much smaller than I'd expected. It looked like an insect. It entered the canyon down in the already-rising shadows and began working back and forth. It appeared to fly so close to the canyon wall that I held my breath a couple of times. It paused and hovered several times and I thought the crew had spotted a downed hiker.

I wish this story had a happy ending, but it doesn't. The rescue helicopter traversed the face as systematically as a crop-duster, gradually rising higher and closer to me. But it never stopped, and eventually it cleared the top of the canyon and flew away. I listened for another half-hour or so (of course I could hear no cries while the helicopter was there) and heard no more voices. It could have been a prank, a trick of the wind and the canyon acoustics, a misunderstanding. Or else there was an injured mountaineer out there somewhere who simply failed to make his location known. I have wondered over the years since whether we heard someone in trouble, someone who did not make it down alive.

I've been wearing bright colors ever since.

Good shoes are next. There is an amazing variety of outdoor, trail, hiking, climbing, working, tracking, hunting, stalking, walking shoes and boots in the marketplace. Some people are purists about what goes on their feet, insisting upon particular shoes for particular activities. I don't believe the type of shoe matters much as long as it has enough tread to grip rock surfaces when they're wet and to dig in and

*good shoes = good hike*

hold in loose dirt. A good hiking shoe also ought to provide enough platform support that the soles of your feet won't become sore from stepping on sharp rocks and that your ankles can't turn easily. Otherwise, I don't think it matters for day hiking whether you wear running shoes or cross-trainers or work boots or traditional leather hiking boots — as long as they're broken in to the point where they are comfortable and will not cause friction, rubbing, and blisters.

For heavy-duty backpacking, when you're carrying a pack that weighs 40 pounds or more and traversing rough mountain terrain for days on end, real traditional mountaineering boots are the order of the day. (See chapter 7 for more information.)

I do most of my day hiking in running shoes or cross-trainers. Choosing a brand is a matter of personal preference, but I usually get something by New Balance simply because they're one of the few manufacturers that offer such shoes in various widths, and I know I can find something comfortable for my extra-wide foot. For most light- to medium-duty hiking, I find that a combination of thick wool socks and lightweight running shoes works all day for as many miles as I want to cover. In wet weather, I switch to a pair of mostly-leather, lightweight, low-cut hikers spritzed with water-repellent.

Now about that bright-colored jacket you're going to wear. If it doesn't really block the wind, doesn't really keep you dry in a shower, doesn't have a big generous heavy-duty zipper with a flap over it, and doesn't have pockets big enough to stow a hat or gloves and a pair of binoculars or a camera, plus film and sunglasses, you probably wasted your money, no matter which brand or style you bought. These characteristics are essential. Other features — a snap-on or roll-up hood, a lining of some kind, and Velcro closers at the wrists — may or may not appeal. Good-quality jackets do cost quite a bit, but if you're enough of a grown-up not to be forgetting the jacket in a bar or a taxi then the cost is worth it, because a well-made nylon windbreaker can last 20 years and more.

On to hats. You hear the oft-preached orthodoxy that you should always wear a hat to help regulate your body temperature, preserve heat in cold weather, ward off sun damage, and so on. I always carry a baseball hat simply because in hot weather it keeps the sweat out of my eyes and in rainy or snowy weather it helps keep my eyeglasses free of raindrops or snowflakes.

As for pants, wear anything but blue jeans. They may be a perennially cool fashion statement in town, but on a hiking trail, looser is always better. Tight-fitting pants, especially those made of a fabric as stiff as denim, bind up around your knees and thighs, and you actually have to work harder to overcome the flex-resistance of such garments. You can really feel the difference when climbing rocks or stretching and crouching as you work your way across very cluttered terrain. The old "stovepipe"-leg work pants function well, and some purpose-built hiking pants with cargo pockets and about 5 percent Spandex for stretchiness work really well.

For most hiking, especially in the forest, over rocky terrain, or anywhere near water, shorts are simply an invitation to bug bites and skinned knees. If it is really, really hot and you're in a flatland area that's dry and the weather won't sneak up on you, it might be okay to wear shorts. But even in this situation, long pants ward off insects, nettles, and cactus spines better than shorts will. They'll also protect the skin on your legs if you have to kneel down to crawl under a fallen tree, have to crawl across a log-bridge, or even suddenly feel the urge to climb a rough-barked tree (more to come on bear-avoidance).

On top, go for layers. Long-sleeved polyester T-shirts and a fleece pullover work well. Some people prefer to wear nothing that needs to be tucked in. If I'm certain I'm not going to be facing wet conditions, I prefer an all-cotton sweatshirt or a cotton flannel long-sleeved shirt — with the tails left out.

## WHAT TO CARRY

As little as possible, as light as possible. You've got to figure that every ounce you're toting gets toted by the expenditure of your very own personal calories. So you want to conserve your energy by limiting just how much tonnage you'll be lugging up those interminable switchbacks.

First, the day pack. For really light going, some people wear just a fanny pack, which has enough room for sunglasses, a small water bottle, and a point-and-shoot camera. This little bundle is okay if you're going out for maybe an hour or two in fairly civilized countryside, but for a full afternoon hike or day hike, I'd be more comfortable carrying more essentials. Of course, if there is more than one person in your hiking party, not everyone needs to carry all the essentials. And of course, what you carry varies with the terrain and the season.

Let's assume you're going solo on a full-day hike. Start with a day pack. Book-bag-sized packs are too small to carry much more than a water bottle, a pocket bird guide, an apple, and a pair of sunglasses. So work with something a little bigger, say in the range of 20 inches x 13 inches x 8 inches, that has at least two outside zipper pockets, one of them large enough to carry a quart-sized water bottle. Mesh pockets are especially handy because they allow you to see a pocket's contents without having to unload it.

internal-frame day pack

The bag should zip shut securely and have two runners on the zipper. (When you zip up, "park" the runners one side or the other but not in the middle; when parked there, the runners tend to work their way down the sides of your pack, a sneaky move that you won't notice until you hear your possessions clattering onto the trail behind you.) Choose a pack in a brilliant, nonnatural color — even if you're from New York and prefer everything black — for the same reasons your jacket ought to be bright.

My favorite day pack — long since worn completely out and discarded — was made of densely woven, water-repellent nylon and had three outside pockets with stout zippers and an inner foam liner that rode against my back. It was thin but dense foam, and it was effective in keeping sharp corners of cameras or books from jabbing me, and it doubled as a comfy seat during lunch breaks in rocky terrain. The pack also had a cowhide bottom; the thick material added weight, but over years of use being dropped, scuffed — even dragged — in rugged country, it did not wear through. It was also a very bright red.

Some day packs now come with reflective strips or panels stitched on, and that seems worthwhile. Some packs also feature waist bands that help distribute the weight, but unless you're transporting boulders out of the backcountry (which is illegal, anyway), they seem to be an unnecessary complication. Just one more thing to undo when you have to take off the pack and fish around for your flashlight.

When checking out the features on a day pack, I would look very carefully at the place where the shoulder straps (padded ones, of course) are stitched to the top of the bag. You should see a large pattern of multiple stitching through the folded-over nylon webbing, and perhaps some gusseting, as well. This is the major point of wear, and I've noticed that when day packs fail — as they will at least once a year under today's standard-issue book load for high school students — that's where they come apart.

For a long solo hike, here's the essential stuff I put in the pack. In fact, a lot of this never leaves my current day pack.

**Water bottle.** Pack at least a quart per person in a bottle that won't leak. Plastic Nalgene "lab" bottles seem to last forever. On hotter days, carry more water. If you're hiking in a desert or another location with scant shade and relentless sunshine, double the amount of water, even if you don't believe you'll need it. You'll need it.

**Sunglasses with UV protection.** I have always worn prescription glasses anyway, and I hate glare, so these are a must.

**Map.** The more detailed, the better. I favor USGS 7.5 maps for their detail; they're readily available at outdoor sports stores. (Here's how long I've been at this: I can remember when the government charged a quarter for those wonderful maps.) You can get waterproof maps of more popular areas like national parks or wilderness areas from publishers like Trails Illustrated. Even if all you have is a Rand-McNally state road map, do carry one; it at least gives the whereabouts of the nearest roads and towns and rivers. (See the next chapter for more details on maps.)

**Tool.** I favor the trusty Swiss Army knife for its blades, punch/awl, tweezers (which are especially useful for desert hiking amidst the dreaded cholla), and, of course, the corkscrew; you never know when you might encounter a good bottle of wine. Some people prefer the kind of multi-tool made by Leatherman and other companies. I find those a bit more weighty and a lot more artillery than I need for day hiking. The point is, you need to have some kind of steel-hard device for such contingencies as having to pry a troublesome nail out of your hiking shoe. You can't do that with a fingernail, a twig, or a rock, so carry a steel tool.

**Matches.** Make sure they're waterproofed, or keep them in a waterproof container.

**Compass.** Not to make a big deal of it (see chapter 5 on navigating), but a compass is small, light, and cheap — you can get a perfectly good one for about $15 — and even if all you do with it is verify which direction you're hiking in every once in a while, it's a good tool to have with you.

**Hat.** For reasons noted previously (see page 50). In winter, make sure it's a warm hat. In wet weather, make sure it has a brim to keep water out of your eyes.

**Additional clothing.** Pack something that will warm you up — a pocket rain jacket, a fleece pullover, a sweatshirt, or a down vest. In winter, I would add a spare pair of socks and a pair of wool gloves.

**Snack.** Or meal, depending on how long I plan to hike. If I'll be on the trail for more than 2 to 3 hours, I pack something substantial. Otherwise, I bring along granola bars, fruit (a banana, orange, or apple), peanut-butter crackers, or a chunk of plain cheddar rat-cheese — something with some caloric value to it.

**Bandanna.** A rag or a couple of paper towels will also do. You just need something to wipe things off with.

**Duct tape.** A small role of this is very handy. You probably could hike twenty times and have no need of it, but for that one time you must tape a flapping sole back onto a disintegrating hiking shoe or patch a rubbed hole in your pack that's threatening to jettison your valuables, there's nothing like duct tape.

**Flashlight.** Any number of small bright lights are on the market. The waterproof models with the tiny, wheat-seed bulbs have appealing traits, but I find the bulbs too fragile and easily damaged, so I prefer the larger bayonet-bulb models, preferably ones powered by alkaline AA batteries. Headlamps are a very handy item when you're camping, as they free up your hands for chores at a campsite after dark. But they're not essential for day hiking.

**First aid kit.** It would be easy to go overboard here and carry enough for minor surgery. Still, you might enjoy a better day if you carry along some padded bandages, a disinfectant solution, a tube of cortisone cream, Sting-eze, some ibuprofen or aspirin, antacid tablets, and adhesive tape. In spring or summer, I might add a "deet"-based insect repellent and sunblock lotion.

## Then comes the fun stuff.

**Binoculars.** I leave the big heavy-duty ones at home and carry a compact model no larger than a deck of cards. They're not great, but they're an improvement over my bifocals.

**Guidebook.** Guidebooks can be heavy, so I carry just one, something that will help me identify birds, trees, shrubs, reptiles, mushrooms, tracks, wildflowers — some aspect of the natural surroundings. For me, a lot of the appeal of hiking has to do with the opportunity to add — informally and painlessly — to my own personal store of knowledge.

**Notebook and pen.** It's not that I can't make a move without taking notes, but sometimes it is useful to write something down so you

*essential sight-seeing gear*

will remember an exact description of it. You can also write down some directions, if navigating becomes a problem. Or you may want to sketch a picture or diagram of something you see, such as small mammal tracks you cannot identify, for checking on later. Or you might be so overcome by the scenery that you simply have to stop and compose a sestina.

**Camera.** Usually I take something simple and light, like a point-and-shoot 35 mm, if I'm heading toward a site I'd like a picture of, just for the flavor of it. Or if I'm hiking with family or friends and we might want pix of us all in situ.

That's it. Except for one thing that should be on your person if not in your pack: a durable timepiece that can be read in the dark and in any weather. (And do take note of the time you set out on the trail.) I also always have a second ignition key somewhere on me or on the car, just on the odd chance that my car keys will get dropped into a roaring torrent or a woodchuck hole.

Other people are known to carry much more, and more specialized, gear, but these are, I believe, the essentials, and they leave room for optional items such as more clothes, more books, a picnic, a groundcloth, hairspray, sandals, toothpicks, candy, a CD player, and any number of other oddments.

## About cell phones: I have two of them for urban and on-the-road use, but I have never carried one on a hike. It's fair to say I hike for reasons that have everything to do with "cell phones not." I like to hike precisely because hiking places me out of touch. Off the grid. I think I will feel that way even when the proliferation of cell-phone towers across our fair land reaches the saturation level at which time it will be possible to make — or worse yet, receive — a phone call when you are sprawled in a state of rapturous fatigue on a sun-warmed boulder on a peak in the White Mountains. Suddenly your cell phone sounds its jarring electronic notes: It might be your best client. It might be your mother. It might be an emergency (which you could do nothing about from up/out here). It might be a tape-recorded voice offering you a swell deal on another credit card.

Under certain dire circumstances, I suppose a cell phone could thwart some inconveniences like getting lost or frostbitten or could assure your timely rescue in the event of an injury. So, when cell phones do begin to work in the kinds of places I like best to hike in, I may not blame other people for carrying a cell, as long as they use it outside of my earshot and only for truly life and death emergencies — which, if you follow the advice of this book and do your hiking *right,* you'll never encounter anyway. So leave the cell at home or in the car. You and I will be better hikers and better people for it.

# five

# Navigating

—

You are here.
And you are supposed
to be there.

IF HIKING IS ESSENTIALLY PUTTING ONE FOOT IN FRONT of the other, then navigating is knowing where your feet are taking you. Sounds simple.

But the question is, when you're hiking along in the Arapaho National Forest, the Cape Cod National Seashore, or Big Bend National Park, *how* do you know where you are at any given moment, and where you're going?

In your everyday life, when you set out to walk to a certain location, how do you know where you're going? If it's a familiar goal, a place you've walked to many times before, you navigate by following familiar visual clues. You see houses, landscaping, signs, street and sidewalk textures, even parked cars and people that you have seen before. But think back to the first time you set out to walk this now-familiar route. Did you follow written or oral directions? Did you check a street map for the accurate arrangement of streets and cross-streets? Or follow the numbers on houses and stores? Perhaps you took note in general terms of compass directions, as in, I'm heading north toward 3400 North Charles Street and I'm in the 1800 block of St. Paul. I know St. Paul is east of Charles, so I need to walk one block west and then about 16 blocks north. In most grid-pattern American cities, that's about all you need to know. You can figure out the directions by the progress of the numbers and perhaps by the sunlight, so you needn't carry a compass or a GPS receiver.

Sometimes, in a city, a suburb, or a semi-rural sprawl area, you need a map to figure out how to get where you're going, and for this reason most of us carry roadmaps in our cars.

A lot of the fun of hiking is exploring, that is to say, going toward a place and seeing it for the first time. Playing with the unknowns, in effect. But seeing it for the first time means there won't be any familiar visual clues along the way, so while it is simplicity itself to hike along a clearly defined trail, it is something else to know where that trail is taking you. And equally important, how long it will take you to get where you want to go. And back.

You can ask directions. It's clear from all the jokes and cliches that some people have issues about stopping to ask directions from a stranger. But personal hang-ups or not, when you ask directions, you want to be sensitive about your sources. When you ask a question like "Where is the nearest trailhead in the Lolo National Forest?" or "Does this trail go all the way to the top of Breakneck Ridge?" most people will tell you. If they know. Sometimes they don't know but want to be helpful so they will guess at the answer or even fake it. Sometimes I have listened to directions that were so obviously wrong, confused, or anomalous that I was reminded of the journalist's dictum: Get at least two sources for the story.

Sometimes the directions you get are suspect for other reasons. Once, I set out to backpack on a segment of the Long Trail in northern Vermont that included, so my sources had indicated, some rare patches of alpine tundra, which I wanted to see. According to my maps, that portion of the Long Trail ran along Robbins Mountain (no relation) located within the boundaries of Camel's Hump State Forest, not far to the southeast of Burlington. It sounded like the place would be simple enough to locate.

Maps can be so beguiling. You look for a state forest on a road map and there it appears, a printed rectangle of green standing out on a background of gray or white, with all the roads and trails clearly labeled. On the map. But then you drive there and the "state forest" does not stand out as a green area because everything in the area is green, heavily forested, and as so often seems to be the case in a New England state, completely innocent of signage. No markings anywhere, except the ones directing me to the nearest Ford dealer. I did the best I could with the road map and a lot of squinting up at the beautiful but inscrutable surrounding green mountains, creeping along the routes that on my map appeared to border the state forest, but I got no information for my efforts.

Time to ask directions. In a very small crossroads village, I stopped where I saw a few people outdoors, husky young men with a lot of facial hair, all of them wearing hats. I had been warned about asking directions in rural New England by another hiker friend, a veteran of several long hikes on the Appalachian Trail. As I approached the young men, I had two thoughts: One concerned the complete reversal in social styles that occurred sometime in the 1970s and persists to this day regarding hair and facial hair. Back then, it was the country boys who were clean-headed as jelly beans and the urban radical hippies who flaunted a lot of long hair, and in situations like the one I was approaching that hippie appearance carried with it the genuine risk of a painful beating. Now the country boys were the ones with the hair and I was safe by virtue of age and demeanor. And shorter hair. The second thought struck when, just as I was about to open my mouth with my question, I spotted a post office. I knew, of course, that *that* was the place to ask for reliable directions, but, alas, it was Sunday and the post office was closed. So I approached. The four men, lounging at the rear of a rusty blue pickup truck, fell silent and turned toward me — the obvious and proverbial stranger. Humorist Jean Shepherd once recounted how he'd found himself in a northern Florida bar where it became obvious that the locals didn't cotton to strangers, adding, "If there's anything I look like, it's a stranger." I knew the feeling.

"I'm looking for an entrance to Camel's Hump State Forest," I said.

No response. Then one shook his head and another asked, "What?"

I repeated, "Camel's Hump State Forest. I'm looking for an entrance road."

The one who'd shaken his head negatively continued to shake his head and said, "Never heard of it."

"Um," I said. "It's a state forest. It's supposed to be near here." I nodded in the direction of the blue-green ridges that loomed over us. "You never heard of it." I was careful to make that a plain statement, not an incredulous or challenging question.

"Nope."

The others shook their heads to indicate they'd never heard of it, either. They were good, I had to admit. There wasn't a trace of a smile among them.

"How about Robbins Mountain?"

More head shaking.

"The Long Trail?"

This one was too well-known even for these guys. One, dressed in a camouflage T-shirt under a flannel long-sleeves — nothing tucked in — nodded up at the long green mountain to my right. "'At's up there. Along the ridge. Don't know what to tell you about how to get up there, though." This was practically a speech. The others looked at him in surprise — whether at the length of the comment or the news that the Long Trail passed through their neighborhood, I couldn't tell.

"Okay, gentlemen," I concluded, as evenly as I could. "Thanks for your help." We could continue this game for as long as it amused them and me, but it wouldn't help me find that patch of alpine tundra. I walked back to my car. The four locals watched in expressionless silence as I started up, put it in gear, and eased past them.

"Woodchucks," I thought, remembering my friend's warning. Clearly I had made their day.

Eventually I found a congenial diner on a larger state road where the personnel were more accommodating to passing strangers. They directed me to a narrow unmarked road that led to a marked trailhead for the Long Trail. And yes, it was located in Camel's Hump State Forest. When I finally reached the trail itself, it was clearly marked, and I had no trouble following it up to that alpine tundra and to a nearby lean-to shelter campsite.

A friend, a historian and archeologist who's done a lifetime of field-work, often told me, "Always make local inquiries." Works for him. But you can't always get what you want out of people. This is another reason to learn how to use maps.

## MAPS

A good, detailed map is the best navigational tool for hiking, and most topographic maps deliver a wealth of information. But maps can be wrong. One caution with the government-issue maps, especially those of the big national forests, is that in some instances the serious, on-the-ground survey work was completed decades ago and was followed by only aerial surveys to pick up the major "cultural" changes like the building of an Interstate highway or the creation of a new open-pit mine. But otherwise, nothing on the map — and that includes decades-old designations of trails — gets checked on the ground or changed on the paper. I learned this the hard way.

Hiking alone in New Mexico's Black Range west of Truth or Consequences and south of the eerie Plains of San Agustin (the site of the railroad-mounted Very Large Array of radiotelescopes), I got lost several times in the space of several days of hiking. *Lost* in these circumstances, I came to realize, is a relative term. It wasn't that in the popular parlance "I had no idea where I was." (I did once get lost so thoroughly in Mexico City that I truly had no idea where I was, except that I was in Mexico City.) I knew, as I hiked along in the open ponderosa pine forest, on a carpet of reddish brown duff, that I was in New Mexico, that I was in the Black Range, that I was in the Gila National Forest, that I was probably about 7,000 feet above sea level, and that I was somewhere west of Winston and Chloride (practically ghost towns then) but had not yet crossed Route 59. At least I didn't think I remembered crossing a paved road . . . I knew I was moving north, more or less (I had a compass to tell me so), and that I was near the top of a meandering broad ridge that was heavily forested and not all that well defined. So I figured from my map that I was more or less walking along the Continental Divide (it's a clear dotted line on most maps, but invisible on the ground).

But as I hiked and looked vainly for clearer signs that I was on a trail, for a blaze on a tree or some other indicator that someone had purposefully walked this way before, I did not know precisely where I was. My best guess was that I was somewhere in a square about ten miles to a side. More specifically than that, I couldn't say.

I was not alarmed. It was a pleasant day with no sign that the weather would turn ugly, and I was not in a hurry to be at a specific spot at a specific hour. I was sort of lost, but I thought, "So what?" It did occur to me that not being more precise about my location than "an area of 100 square miles" would sound thoroughly and alarmingly lost to most people. To someone in familiar urban surroundings, say back east in New York, it would sound nearly hopeless.

But on that sunny day in the Black Range, being lost wasn't much more than an annoyance. It just meant I could waste a lot of hours — even a day or two — and a lot of energy if I was not more direct about my travel and my eventual rendezvous with my parked van. When I started out, I had followed the trail for a while, but it seemed imperceptibly to become less well-defined, then ambiguous, and finally to disappear. I couldn't say precisely where, among the ponderosa pine and Douglas fir in this spacious forest, the trail had turned or faded or just stopped. Twice I saw very old blazes well up on trees — probably done by the Civilian Conservation Corps (CCC) trail crews in the 1930s, from the look of them — but when I circled out in a spiraling, widening pattern, checking trees all the while, I failed to find a next blaze. So, no trail.

I had a lot of time to think about trails on that day. When you look at a map, they seem so clear and unambiguous, so firmly placed that it's easy to forget that what's on the map is a symbol that someone drew on a sheet of paper, and what may or may not be out on the ground in a particular real forest is something else altogether. Trails may have traversed this section of forest once, but perhaps they were used so little that they faded away. To be honest, the terrain I was traveling was hot, dry, and rather monotonous, due to its sheer vastness. When you're on foot in the West, the distances work a qualitative effect on your experience: The dry green ridges of forest seem to go on forever under the

*"lost" in the Black Range of New Mexico*

hot and timeless New Mexico sunshine. The scent of the pines pervades every step and every moment, riding on the hot wind that rises up from the broad shallow valleys below. On a long summer afternoon, time seems to stop, distances waver uncertainly in the shimmering heat, and it seems altogether fitting that on a plain just north of here, there are enormous devices aimed at studying eternal space.

So I wandered from side to side of a compass bearing somewhat to the west of north, kept putting one foot in front of another, and rather relished being lost — slightly lost, that is, within a set area. Somewhat past my usual dinner time, I started down a short slope and spotted the dark pavement of Route 59. I was out of the box.

During the period I was lost, I didn't do a lot of navigating, per se. But what I also did not do was become anxious or panicky at the thought of being lost. Being lost, by itself, is not a hazardous or threatening state.

It is a mental state. I was, after all, *somewhere*. I just could not pinpoint that somewhere at that time. It's the panic and unreasoning imprudent actions that occur in the state of panic that cause the harm.

Before you rely fully on a detailed map — either a hiking map produced by the agency that administers the land on which you are hiking or a standard-issue USGS 7.5 minute topographic map (also known as a "Quad" map) — take the time to read and understand the information on the map. A 7.5 topo map displays about 45 square miles of terrain, showing elevations and elevation changes in terms of contour lines at various intervals; roads from Interstate highways to unimproved dirt roads, plus some (but not all) trails; buildings, railroads, power lines, strip mines, dams, cemeteries, and other "cultural" features; water, such as swamps, occasional streams, rivers, farm ponds, and lakes; and some land-use features, whether open country (e.g. farm fields), orchards, or forest cover. These maps also include a distance scale in feet (an inch equals 2,000 feet), miles, and kilometers; latitude and longitude; the dates of publication and revisions; plus some administrative information like names of townships and counties.

I find these maps irresistible, crammed with fascinating revelatory information about the whole American countryside, and as such wonderfully entertaining documents for planning a hike and even armchair hiking. As in, "Look, if we park the car here and hike about a mile up through the forest to that old fire tower we'll probably get great views of the valley to the west. Then we can hike along the ridge to this old dirt road and down past this farm to the county road. And we'll come out within hiking distance from where we left the car." I just love these maps.


## BLAZES

Many trails on public lands that see a lot of recreational use are *blazed*. Blazes usually consist of a rectangle of paint, approximately 4 inches x 6 inches, applied at eye level or above to trees, and occasionally to fences or rocks. Some trails are blazed with metal medallions nailed to trees. Blazes are usually placed so that when you are standing directly before one blaze, the next one is plainly visible down the trail. In poor light, in difficult weather, or on a trail obscured by brush, leaves, or snow, make certain you can spot the next blaze before moving on.

In areas where it is not possible to mark a trail with painted blazes — above tree line, for instance — trails are sometimes marked by small neat heaps of stones, called *cairns*. When you're hiking along at alpine altitudes in, say, the Sierra Nevada, you may find that these small pyramids are the only sign of a trail.

Blazes are generally applied by the agency that manages the land, be it BLM, NPS, or a state department of conservation, or by a private recreational organization or club like the Appalachian Mountain Club

*eye-level trail blaze*

or a college outing club. During the 1930s a lot of trail miles were cleared and blazed by the federal Civilian Conservation Corps.

There is something reassuring about following a blazed trail; it conveys a sense that someone who was familiar with the trail passed this way and left behind clear markers. But some cautions apply. In many areas, a large network of trails cross and recross each other, leading off in all directions, with the various trails marked by different-colored blazes. Without a map that shows a key to the trail colors, it's impossible to tell which color is the one you ought to follow.

Following blazes raises the issue of trail junctions. When you're navigating by means of a trail map, your most important duty is to pay attention to trail junctions. Whenever you come to a crossing of trails, stop and read your map, and check the compass direction against the direction of the trails themselves. It is very easy to get distracted and miss a trail junction or take the wrong one and discover your error miles and hours later — especially if you're hiking in a talkative group. In any group, it should be everyone's responsibility to take note of all the trail junctions and all the blazes.

## COMPASS

*Indispensable* is the word for a compass. People have been finding their way around the world with only a compass for centuries. Paired with a decent map, a compass can get you un-lost every time. And in the wilderness, low-tech is more reliable than high-tech, so rely on a plain magnetic/mechanical compass rather than an electronic one (batteries can die).

There are a lot of ways to use a compass, but here are the basics: First, learn how to use the compass before you set out for a hike with it. At home, get out a topo map and pick out a trail, a trailhead, and an objective. Put the compass on the map and "box" it, that is, rotate the dial until you see a straight line between the trailhead and the objective, and read that direction off the compass in degrees. For example, if you are

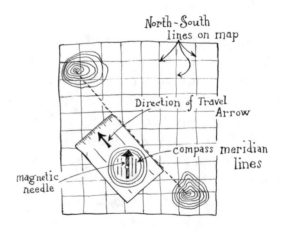

*boxing a compass*

hiking along the Appalachian Trail in eastern Pennsylvania and you are joining the trail at Lehigh Gap near Palmerton, from Route 248, and you intend to hike to the next highway, Route 115 at Wind Gap, your compass will tell you that you should hike east-northeast at a bearing of about 65 degrees.

Bear in mind that a compass points to the magnetic north, not true north. The difference between the two, called *declination,* varies depending on where on the continent you are located. The declination is essentially zero in the Mississippi Valley and increases as you move east or west from there. Declination is usually shown in degrees on a detailed map, such as a USGS 7.5 minute map.

When you get to a trailhead, check the compass against your map and the terrain and determine the approximate bearing to your day's objective. Of course, if you are in hilly, wild terrain, it won't be possible — or from the standpoint of an interesting hike, desirable — to hike in a straight line. So check your heading from time to time as you follow the trail. And check it every time you come to a trail junction or have to detour around an obstacle like a hill or a river crossing.

It's possible to get much more refined and detailed about navigating with a compass by taking and noting precise bearings each time you change directions even slightly. But for most day hiking in the lower 48 states, that's not necessary. To guard against getting lost, it's only essential to know that, outbound, you hiked to the northeast and therefore to return you should hike to the southwest.

## GPS

Global Positioning System receivers, which combine a radio receiver with a tiny computer, can, under the right circumstances, pinpoint your location to an accuracy of within about 50 feet. They work by receiving three or four of the signals beamed down from 24 satellites placed in orbit by the United States government, computing your position by triangulation, and projecting the results in terms of coordinates or on a graphic display map. The GPS tells you "You are here." The system was set up originally for military use and then extended to civilian use.

A GPS receiver can be useful, but consider some caveats: While hiking, you may be in a location where your receiver cannot pick up enough satellite signals to calculate your position. Also, a GPS receiver is an electronic device, subject to the real-world hazards of being dropped, lost, stepped on, wet, and otherwise broken. The receiver operates on battery power, and you know what that means: batteries have a pernicious tendency to fade out just when you need them most. In my opinion, in wild country (or on big wild water) a GPS receiver is not a substitute for a traditional compass and a good map.

If you're going to have a GPS receiver with you, then, as with map and compass, first learn how to use it at home under low-stress conditions. The last hour of daylight when you have gotten your hiking party lost in the wilderness is not the time to haul out the GPS owner's manual and try to figure out which buttons to push and what all those little numbers mean.

## BUSHWHACKING

How important is it to stick to a trail? I've been asked this question often, and not always by kids. The answer depends on how much distance you're covering, how familiar you and your party are with the area, the weather, the light and time of day, and, of course, the nature of the terrain. In one of the open, parklike, mid-altitude ponderosa or Douglas fir groves in the western mountains, where there is scant understory and you know there are no intervening surprise ravines or flash-flooding creeks, the potential for trouble is low. The same might be said if you're hiking across meadowlands and your goal is in sight. Otherwise, stay on the trail.

For some people, "staying on the trail" is kind of a red flag to their bullish self-assertion, reminiscent of childhood injunctions against coloring outside the lines. Tramping around hillsides, boulder fields, or wetlands without paying any mind to trails, markers, or other signs of civilized activity does carry with it an appealing sense of freedom. So without listing all the possible pratfalls, I will just note that there are multiple potential prices to be paid for that sense of freedom, and that trails are generally the easiest way to go in wild terrain. That's why they exist in the first place; trails usually define the path of least resistance.

One other point: If the subject of navigation holds no appeal for you, definitely stay on the trail. In most recreational areas where the trails are well used and well maintained, the only act of navigation you need to commit to is simply staying on the trail. If that's all you do, you'll have minimal need even for a compass or map.

## READING THE NATURAL SIGNS

Should a situation ever arise when for whatever reason — a capsized canoe, a pack lost over the edge of a cliff, or an act of plain stupidity — you find yourself out in the wild at the end of a day's hike uncertain about where you are, exactly, and which way you should go, there are a few things to keep in mind. Lest you spend a miserable night on Bald Mountain.

First, if you are lost and truly have no clear notion about which way to go, don't go anywhere. Stay in one place until you have figured out a reasonable plan either for reaching civilization or for waiting until someone finds you. Above all, do not start casting about in random fashion if twilight is nigh. Thrashing around in the dark in unknown terrain is a direct route to personal injury.

Think first about whether anyone else knows approximately where you are (they do if you bothered to tell them before your hike), and whether you're enhancing your chances of someone locating you if you stay put. If this is the case, then definitely stay where you are. If you can find a clearing nearby, establish there some markers that can be seen from an aircraft. Three of anything is the international standard call for help, so place three distinct crossed logs, piles of gear, unnaturally shaped brush piles, or bright garments where they can be seen from above.

If you can reason your way to the appropriate direction for you to head — due west, say, to reach a roadway that can't be more than eight miles away — wait until you have plenty of light (such as the next morning) before moving out. And don't make a move until you have figured out how, once you're moving, you're going to keep heading in the right direction in a more-or-less straight line. This way, you don't just wander witlessly in a circle (it happens!), burning up much-needed energy and body warmth. Be sure to consider the weather in your calculations of what to do. You don't want to add, say, hypothermia to your predicament.

Try to remember from your map reading any information you can about the general shape of the nearby country and the locations of such important landmarks as roads, towns, power-transmission lines, airfields, rail lines, and any other natural or cultural features that might help you figure out where you are in relation to where you need to go. The lonesome wail of a distant freight train, the vector of a descending aircraft, or the location of a blinking warning light on a distant tower could be the clue that gets you correctly oriented. Pay attention, and think! I once navigated through miles of Mexico City to the major airport, despite having no Spanish, by following the direction of descending jetliners until I began seeing some with their landing gear down. Then I knew I was getting "warm."

Before you move in any direction from where you were standing when anxiety attacked, try to establish compass direction. If it's a clear day, where is the sun and where is it coming up or going down? This can give you a rough idea of east and west. If it's a clear night, where is the Big Dipper, which points to the North Star? If the sky is solidly overcast and you can't really see the sun, stand in a clearing and check to see if you are casting any sort of shadow. If you are, you can locate the sun, and if you know about what time it is, you can point to east and west.

If it's raining or snowing, you may be able to make an informed guess about directions. If you're in the Northeast and it's raining, note where the rain is blowing in from; in the Northeast, for example, rain often comes either directly out of the west or out of the northeast, but rarely from the north. In most places on the continent, snow rarely blows out of the south; it much more frequently comes from the west, northwest, or north. Taking your direction from precipitation is not a sure thing, but it is a clue.

If you cannot recall or observe any detail or scrap of information that would suggest the best direction to move in, choose a direction based on terrain. If you can see more vegetation — thicker brush, taller trees (especially if they're in a line), or just more darkness against the background — consider heading in that direction. Thicker brush often signifies the presence of water, and as all plumbers know, water runs downhill. This can be important. If you follow the course of water downhill, it most likely will lead to a bigger body of water, and from there an even bigger body of water — say from a creek to a river — and at some point all that water is likely to lead you to civilization.

Similarly, if you are up at some elevation, hike downhill, if you can. Most civilized stuff — the roads, railroads, navigable waters, and settlements — can be found on the flat and level parts of the world. Keep going downhill, and eventually you will reach something useful. Of course, this rule of thumb has some caveats: If you are in the kind of terrain where there is any reason to suspect sudden drop-offs, do not hike in poor light or darkness, for obvious reasons. I once walked away from a Colorado campsite above tree line that had almost no distinctive features and was close to several high drop-off cliffs. I had gone no more than 200 yards when the wind shifted and brought in a cloudbank so dense that I could see no more than six feet in any direction. I shouted out and my wife, back at camp, responded, but it took at least 30 minutes of gospel-like shouts and responses to talk me slowly but safely back through the fog to camp.

Also, in some parts of the country, especially in the eastern mountains, many slopes lead downhill to coves or closed valleys. You could walk downhill into one of these and find nothing but more woods, wildness, and darkness, with no egress to anything civilized.

As you hike toward what you hope is civilization, stop frequently to listen for any cultural sounds and to look around for any lights on the horizon or light-scatter in the sky that indicates the location of a town.

In general, a few simple *pre*-cautions, like the ones mentioned here, can relieve your mind of worries about getting lost. In most day-hiking situations on established trails on public land, navigating is simple and getting lost is rarely an issue. In backcountry wilderness, it's worth thinking about in advance.

# six

# Cautions

—

In the wilderness, we don't get scared —
we get concerned.

ONCE, AFTER RETURNING FROM A THREE-WEEK CAMP-ing and hiking trip in the Rocky Mountains, I encountered a neighbor who was something of an outdoorsman and did some fishing and deer-hunting in central Pennsylvania. When I mentioned that I had just come back from hiking alone in some mountainous wilderness areas and camping out alone in a high desert area, he responded that he "could never do that." Surprised, I asked why. His answer was a bit evasive, but it was clear that he thought being out alone in the wild was madly dangerous. "There's nothing out there that can really hurt you," I said. "It's nothing to be afraid of." He gave me a look and just shook his head.

I've often recalled that conversation, and I've since decided that my answer was too simple and too glib. I sensed that my neighbor imagined that something, some big hairy critter, might be out there to *get* him. But I knew that the only wild animals out there to worry about — apart from venomous snakes, which are readily fended off by good boots — were grizzly bears. I also knew how rare it is to see a grizzly, even when you are in prime bear habitat in the two places in the lower forty-eight where they roam in greatest numbers: Glacier and Yellowstone. And how much rarer it is to encounter a grizzly that does not simply rumble off at the sight or sounds or smell of human hikers. Cases of humans actually being attacked by grizzly bears are incredibly rare. Hikers are much more likely to be struck by lightning, to drown crossing a swift stream, or to die in an SUV wreck on their way to or from a hiking trail than to be attacked by *Ursus horribilis.*

I wasn't quite fair in answering that neighbor, because there are some things about hiking in the wild that I *am* concerned about. Not afraid, mind you, but *concerned.* They are concerns that I think any hiker ought to consider without letting them compromise the rewards of hiking. They apply chiefly to hiking in wild country and are much less important if you are day-hiking in a comparatively civilized place like a small local wildlife refuge or a popular state park.

My hiking concerns are sixfold: weather, distance (especially in the West), illness, other hikers, a few annoying critters, and above all, my own propensity for folly.

## WEATHER

As part of the universe's grand indifference to your schedule and fun, it can rain on your parade. Or snow on it, flood it out, hit it with lightning, pelt it with hail, freeze it, or burn it. Weather can change very rapidly, especially at high altitudes and in certain seasons and conditions. People who know they will be in a hazardous environment far from immediate help, like commercial fishermen, pay elaborate attention to the weather and to weather forecasts. So should hikers. And if the weather looks volatile, hike another day. This is especially important in areas where the terrain may magnify the weather and contribute to powerful consequences, such as a steep ravine where flash floods could

*rain gear*

occur, an alpine zone that draws lightning like a magnet, or a desert zone where direct sun can elevate temperatures to extraordinary degrees.

I have hiked through every kind and change of weather except a hurricane and suffered no more than brief discomfort, largely because I always bring extra items of clothing — dry socks, a baseball hat, wool gloves, a layer of something warm, and a rainproof jacket — that can ward off at least some of what an ugly sky can drop on me. Extra clothing, some of it water-repellent, is about all you need to stay comfortable in most bad-weather situations.

Lightning can be a significant risk to hikers, particularly if you're hiking in an exposed area. If a thunderstorm is blowing up fast and you can't avoid it, seek shelter in a dense grove of trees that has no really tall trees standing up like lightning rods. Don't be the tallest object in the area; in other words, get out of a large open field, get down off an exposed ridge line, or get off the water.

Thunder is a good indicator of how close you are to a lightning strike. When a thunderstorm is approaching, count the number of seconds between the flash of lightning in the sky and the sound of its thunder, then divide by five to figure the number of miles between you and the storm. If your count is, say, thirty seconds, divide by five and you learn that the lightning strike was six miles away. If your count is in the area of ten seconds or less, the strike was just two miles away or less. Seek shelter immediately.

Sometimes there are other powerful indications that a lightning strike is about to occur. I was once hiking up a mountainside with a seasonal ranger who was on fire lookout duty in Glacier National Park when we were overtaken above the tree line by a fast-moving storm. As the cold rain suddenly hit us, he shouted that if I felt a buzzing or felt my hair standing up, it was a sign that lightning could strike soon, and I should drop to the ground but stay in a crouch on my feet.

In high dry forests like the Black Range in New Mexico, not only is lightning directly dangerous, but it also starts forest fires. One night when I camped out in the Black Range, a passing violent thunderstorm started a number of forest fires — over forty in a single night in the Gila National Forest, I later learned from a ranger. Luckily, none of them approached the area where I was camping.

Most small fires can be readily avoided. At the first signs of smoke or that acrid burning smell, try to determine the location and speed of the fire and the direction it's moving in. Fires move with the wind and move more rapidly uphill than on the level. If you can, retreat to the trailhead and your vehicle; otherwise, get to the nearest road or parking area or any place that offers a minimum of fuel to a fire. As soon as you can, report the fire to the local authorities. (And above all, do not be the cause of a fire.)

Other weather-related conditions to be mindful of include thirst and dehydration, hypothermia, and frostbite. These conditions can readily be forestalled by a few smart hiking precautions, such as carrying plenty of drinking water, dressing appropriately for the weather, and carrying a rainproof jacket and some extra warm clothing (including socks).

## DISTANCE

My reading of the literature suggests that most commercial airliner crashes can be attributed to a combination of factors, including maintenance mistakes, mechanical malfunctions, instrument glitches, pilot error, and plain bad luck. No one of these things commonly brings an aircraft down, but a combination of them can have serious consequences. The case is similar for hiking. No one problem usually gets hikers into serious trouble, but combinations of them can add up to unpleasantness and maybe crisis. Distance is one of those factors; it can complicate any other problem you might encounter and can by itself wear you out. Distance is especially a factor in the mountains and deserts of the West, where everything is so spread out. Read the literature on pioneering settlers who ventured out past the 100th meridian. Nearly every problem they encountered was exacerbated by the sheer distances they were facing. And that was before interstate highways.

Once while hiking in the desert flats west of the Alamo Hueco Range in the boot-heel region of New Mexico, my friend Paul and I were discussing snakes. Several locals — a cowboy friend of Paul's and a border patrol officer — had warned us to watch our step, because the sage flats we were walking through concealed a lot of rattlesnakes. We wore heavy-duty boots, I carried and swung a walking stick, and we certainly kept our eyes and ears open. We'd both heard rattlers before and knew what to listen for. As we talked, we realized that if one of us were struck by a snake, we could be in trouble simply due to *distance*. At the time we were talking, we figured that we were about eight hours from our parked vans, even at a brisk hiking pace. Our vehicles were on an iffy gravel ranch road, at least 20 slow miles from the nearest pavement. Once on a highway, we would be still some 100 miles from the nearest medical help of any kind, and probably that far from the nearest telephone. That's a long distance. It was a sobering thought and led us to scan the rabbit brush and sage even more carefully. (This episode was, perhaps obviously, unfolding in the days before anyone had deployed cell phones or even effective lightweight walkie-talkie radios.) Thankfully, nothing unpleasant happened on that trip. We hiked for many hot, dusty miles and saw a lot of cattle, but no snakes.

The most serious difficulty I ever got myself into on a hike, and the only occasion on which I thought I might die out there, occurred on a glorious clear-sky summer afternoon just north of Logan Pass in Waterton-Glacier International Peace Park. I didn't encounter a grizzly, lightning, or a flash flood. I encountered my own poor judgment in a situation made vastly worse by the vast distances involved. I was hiking alone (not necessarily a fine idea) and became impatient with how long it was taking me to get back to Logan Pass. I was overconfident of my condition, my gear, and my ability to navigate cross-country. I decided to leave the trail and bushwhack more directly to the pass, which I knew was south of me and within five miles.

*taking a "shortcut" from the Highline Trail*

I studied my map of the hiking trails of Glacier and located what appeared to be a far shorter and more direct route than that of the Highline Trail, which I was on. I could see from the contours that it involved crossing a couple of ravines, but they didn't look all that deep or steep. So I left the trail and struck out due south. In that area, Glacier is mountainous, near tree line, and very rugged. The land I was passing through was open, grassy, and rocky, without much in the way of tree cover. I could see plainly the peak of Mount Reynolds, which rises over the south side of Logan Pass, so keeping myself pointed in the right direction was not a problem. And the weather was great. Off I went.

It was easy going until I came to the edge of a small ravine, which was maybe 100 feet deep. I checked for a route down to the talus-strewn bottom and stared at the far side. It was a steep, but not sheer, descent. The floor was sloping but clear, and scrambling up the far side did not appear to be much of a challenge. I looked long enough to identify a likely path down; there seemed to be enough ledges — almost a narrow trail — and handholds to make a quick descent possible. I could either take the plunge and clamber down or backtrack all the way to the Highline Trail and go around, adding at least another hour or two to the hike. Without further consideration, I started down.

The rock face offered good footing and plenty of handholds, and I easily worked my way about halfway down. The rock was a rather crumbly sedimentary variety — not the kind of material a serious rock climber likes to work with. The joke I'd heard was that to go climbing in Glacier "you have to hold the rocks together."

A chimney formation stopped me. It was wider than any such gap had looked from above, and I could not either stretch across or make a leap. But at this point it wouldn't have been easy to turn and climb back up, either. I stood balanced on the narrow ledge, carefully examining the possible handholds and places to put my feet. At one point I would have to stretch around the edge of the chimney, feel for a foothold with my left boot, and then — assuming I'd find one — shift my right hand from one hold to another. I made my move, and it worked out well at first: I found a foothold for my left foot. But when I shifted my weight to the left hand so I could move my right hand to the second grip, the rock under my left hand pulled loose from the face and brought a shower of large rocks with it. For one bad instant, I thought I might be knocked completely loose from the ledge and fall backward some 40 feet to the tangle of boulders and talus below. But I held on with my right hand, stretched out my left foot, and did not fall. However, the bushel or so of football-size rocks plus one about the size of a bucket were trapped between my front and the rock face. I had to ease them away and drop them without dropping myself. I got rid of the smaller rocks and wedged the one big one back into the crack.

Now what? With the sequence of handholds and footholds disrupted, I had to think of something else. I knew I couldn't take long to figure out an answer or I would start losing strength, grip, and maybe nerve and clarity of mind. I started sweating, and I started feeling — very powerfully — a cold fear. I was angry with myself for moving stupidly into this predicament, and I wished I were somewhere else just then. But I couldn't spend much time thinking about anything except the way out. I got very focused. Real danger — to me a curious almost *liquid* feeling of dread — does clear the mind. I knew the only way I was going to get down without painful injury was to solve the problem of that convoluted, crumbling rock face ahead of me.

I studied the chimney and calculated that my best shot would consist of turning around and placing my back to the rock face, shifting my feet so I could stretch across with my right foot to a promising-looking foothold, and then pivoting briskly around so I could again face the rock wall and find grips for my left hand and foot. But I was wearing a substantial backpack, and the only way I would be able to turn around would be to get rid of the pack. I didn't have time to hesitate or ruminate, because I was going to start losing strength soon. I unbuckled my pack, mentally checked its contents, then slipped it off my back. I thought it would simply drop the 40 feet or so and stop, but instead it fell on some boulders and then bounced and bounded on down the talus slope, end over end over end. It looked like a small body dressed in bright yellow and brown. I was uncomfortably surprised. Evidently the talus slope was a good deal steeper than it looked from here. My pack finally came to rest about a quarter-mile down. I couldn't help thinking that, if I fell, I would tumble just as roughly down that slope.

Time for me to make my move. I shifted my feet, placing them carefully, and was able to turn around. I checked the solidity of my handholds and then, without hesitating, stretched out my right leg, found the small ledge — found it *solid,* as I had hoped — and launched into a pivot. In one heart-stopping moment, my right foot started to slide, and I realized that I was wearing my oldest and most worn-out hiking boots, which had almost no tread left. Another of those little factors that contribute to a crash. But I bore down hard with my foot and my boot held, so I completed the swing-around onto a ledge with good grippy handholds. I took a moment to enjoy the feeling of safety, then continued on, easily finding handholds and footholds the rest of the way down to the bottom of the ravine.

Once down, I spent some time just sitting, just breathing, looking from the rock face to the large, edgy boulders at its foot and on down to my pack lying in the sun. I thought about the mistakes I'd made, how stupid and cocky I'd been. But most of all, I thought about space. About distances. Glacier is a million acres of wilderness, jagged mountains and dense forest, 40 miles from one end to the other. That day, I was hiking only about eight miles, and yet the distances in Glacier were such that if I had peeled off that cliff and broken my leg or my head, I could have lain there in plain sight of Logan Pass — nearly in sight of the parking lot where my van was — but well beyond anyone's earshot until I died. Sitting there, I realized that no one on the trail or in the parking lot was likely to have seen me or heard me hollering. No one would have known where to start looking for me because I had strayed so far off the Highline Trail. A potentially lethal combination of factors came together in that place: my own folly, and an intractable distance.

Don't make my dumb mistakes. Make your own. And bear in mind the words of the German poet Johann Schiller: "Against stupidity, the very gods/Themselves contend in vain."

## ILLNESS

I and most every hiker I know has gotten sick out on a trail at some point, and it's an unpleasant setback. Again, the *pre*-cautions are important. Bring your own water, bring some aspirin, bring a bandanna.

About the water: America's wild waters are now so universally polluted, sad to say, that the chances of your hiking alongside a stream sparkling with safe potable water range from slim to zilch. I have twice landed in a hospital from drinking what I imagined was good water. The wild waters of America are beautiful, beguiling, inspiring, and often awe-inspiring. But they are not fit to drink, so look and listen and feel but do not taste.

If you start to feel ill while on a trail, turn around and head back immediately. Don't try to tough it out or wait it out. Your bad feeling may be nothing, but if it's something that rates a couple of paragraphs in a medical manual, minutes count, and you'll be very glad you turned homeward as soon as possible. When you're feeling bad internally (as opposed to, say, having muscle aches), hiking will do nothing but make you feel worse and place you even farther from help.

## OTHER HIKERS

During the hunting seasons in the fall, it's a good idea to be especially cautious of your fellow man, especially if he is in the act of hunting "varmints," deer, elk, bear, or large birds. Hunting accidents are not uncommon. Know the dates of hunting seasons in whichever state you hike in. If you must be out in a forest or field during a hunting season, be certain to wear bright colors — blaze orange is probably most effective and is often worn by the hunters themselves. My own preference (and advice) is simply to stay out of the woods and off the trails during hunting seasons. In an environment in which visibility is often compromised by foliage and weather, the mere notion of people armed with rifles, shotguns, or even bows and arrows who are motivated by a desire to kill an animal has a chilling effect on my passion for hiking. Hunting seasons are, in the great scheme of things, comparatively short. Consider it a good interval to stay home and read books like this.

Hunters aren't the only people you should be wary of. Wearing a primary-color day pack and professing a love of the sunshine and great views does not make a person kind, upright, or law-abiding. Be not deceived: Among the millions of Americans out hiking on a summer day, some are lawless and dangerous. Crime occurs on the bucolic trails of the American wilderness, just as it does in the streets and homes of our "civilized" centers. Experienced rangers in the big wild parks and forests can tell you all about it. This doesn't mean you need to be paranoid, fearful, or unfriendly to whomever you meet on the trail. It does mean you ought not park your normal everyday-life cautions and people-reading skills back at the trailhead.

Once my friend Paul and I were hiking with my teenage daughter Molly in a large remote wilderness at the south edge of Yellowstone and the north edge of the Teton Wilderness. We were joined from a side trail by a slender young man toting a green backpack. He looked to be about

25, was alone, and seemed polite. He introduced himself with just a first name and fell in with us. And we didn't like him one bit. Call it vibes, intuition, paranoia, or whatever you want, but we all felt immediately that there was something odd and creepy about the guy. The first chance I got, I hissed to Paul, "Don't let this guy get between us and Molly." Paul nodded. He'd picked up the same feeling. We hiked along, talking warily. The guy asked a lot of questions about things like what kind of car we had and where we'd left it, and he volunteered only the vaguest answers about where he'd been, what he was doing, and where he was going. And Paul and I both sensed — as we discussed later — that what he did say about where he'd been and how long he'd been out on the trail did not jibe with his appearance or his gear. Something just wasn't right. We hiked on, making friendly conversation, but watching him closely all the while.

In the end, nothing happened. We finished our hike and parted company at the trailhead at about dinner time. But I still believe we were smart to be alert and cautious with that stranger. Reading people accurately is the best way to stay safe in big cities. Works on the trail, too.

## CRITTERS

Depending on where you're hiking, you may encounter nuisance bugs and dangerous bugs. Mosquitoes are both. Ants, except the fire ants of the Southwest, are a nuisance. Flies are mostly a nuisance, though black flies in late spring and early summer in the North are so much a nuisance that they can dangerously alter hiker behavior. (They drive people crazy!) Ticks are dangerous, especially the tiny deer ticks. I have often been host to ticks and luckily have not contracted Lyme disease. It's a good idea to take some tick-preventive cautionary steps. Any time you are hiking in weather warm enough to accommodate insects, apply repellent that contains about 30 percent deet. Wear long sleeves and long trousers (unless you are in stifling heat or some other vital reason compels you to wear shorts and short sleeves — and a burning desire to get tan does not count as a compelling reason). If you are moving through tall grass or brushing through underbrush, stop frequently to check for

# Trail Etiquette

Almost everyone who writes about the outdoors rhapsodizes about "trackless wilderness" or "unspoiled nature" or the "undiscovered country." But while there are such places here and there, the idea of virgin forests is mostly a conceit, a reassuring illusion. The reality is that we live on a continent with nearly 300 million people, many of them restless, mobile, and keen on outdoor recreation. So when you are hiking along a forest trail surrounded by unmarked trees, shrubs, and wildflowers, apparently surrounded by nothing that is non-natural, nothing that shows the hand or foot of humans except the trail itself, consider yourself the beneficiary of many previous careful hikers — and by all means, pass the favor along to future hikers.

In short, leave the place alone and untouched. Leave no sign that you ever passed through this place. Responsible hiking is stealth hiking. That means:

• Anything you bring into the woods should come back out with you. Do we have to mention it? Don't litter.

• Do not pick, pluck, collect, acquire, gather, chop, bother, harass, chase, kill, or eat anything that's already there. Especially anything living.

• Stay on the trails and watch where you place your feet.

• Do not burn anything. If you must start a fire for reasons of hypothermia or rescue, build it only in a clear, bare area with dry downed wood; keep it small; and have the means to extinguish it ready at hand before you start.

• Do not do anything to affect the quality of any water.

• Always move as quietly as possible. That way, you won't compromise the experience of other nearby hikers and you won't spook the wildlife — therefore you will see and hear more of the life around you.

ticks at your ankles, waist, arms, shoulders, and neck. Once I pushed through about 50 feet of fir thicket in the foothills above the Red Desert in Wyoming and, upon inspection, found that I had picked up three ticks on my shirt. I removed them carefully with the tweezers from my Swiss Army knife, then squashed them.

*black bear*

Although you will probably see more insects than anything else, be mindful of the other critters of the wild. One of the great joys of hiking is observing wild animals in their everyday surroundings and movements. But it's important to know how to behave when you encounter a wild animal in the wild. As soon as they become aware of you, most animals will move away as soon as possible. If you stay calm, stay quiet, make no sudden moves, and keep your mouth shut, you will likely get a chance to observe the animal for a bit longer.

Very few animals are dangerous unless provoked. Don't shout at an animal, approach it, or toss things at it. Don't, in short, do anything to frighten the animal or make it feel cornered or challenged.

If you surprise a bear — as I did once in California's Sierra Nevada near a roaring creek that was so noisy that neither of us heard the other approaching — back slowly away. If the bear advances, talk softly to it, but try not to make eye contact or make any moves that could be construed as aggressive. Sometimes bears advance toward people simply to see what they are; bears have a well-developed sense of smell but don't see all that well. Don't run. Bears are like dogs: If you run, they will chase you — and no matter how swift a sprinter you are, a bear is faster.

If you encounter other large animals, such as moose or elk, don't approach or crowd them. Watch quietly and move slowly away. If you are in a forest, try to keep a substantial tree between you and the animal. In really dense and wild settings, wild cats (cougars and lynxes) and wolves may be present, but while day-hiking you are about as likely to encounter one of these powerful predators at close range as you are to win the lottery. They are shy and reclusive and will avoid you.

My neighbor was about half right. You should be cautious about some things when you're in the wild. On the other hand, there is plenty to be cautious about in daily life, too, so keep these hiking cautions in perspective. At home, while traveling, or in strange cities, it is only necessary to exercise your common sense, not to catalog all possible threats from car accidents to muggings, power-line collapses, exploding manhole covers, mad dogs, banana peels, falling cornices, random shootings, volcanic eruptions, earthquakes, and tornadoes. Bad stuff can happen, to be sure, but no more so while hiking than while covering your appointed daily rounds.

*rattlesnake*

# seven

# Backpacking

—

You can take it
with you, but only if
it's very light.

THE SMARTEST SINGLE THING I EVER LEARNED ABOUT backpacking came as a suggestion from my photographer friend and frequent hiking companion Paul Chesley. On one of the first backpacking jaunts we took together, in Waterton-Glacier International Peace Park, we arrived at a likely campsite late in the afternoon on a cloudy day. The campsite was deep in a wilderness forest; we were surrounded by Engelmann spruce and lodgepole pines, without any of the stunning long and deep vistas that generally make Glacier such an irresistible place. Out for a projected five or six days and nights, carrying a heavy load of food and gear, we'd hiked some seemingly endless hot uphill stretches of trail. As always on a first day out, we'd both made some unpleasant discoveries about our gear — the fit of our hiking boots (mine were not as well broken in as I'd thought), the arrangement of sharp-edged photo equipment in our packs, and little annoyances like how inaccessible my water bottle was and how his zipper was prone to jamming. At that moment, when we shucked off our packs and stood staring at the almost-level clearing we'd chosen for our campsite, backpacking felt like not a cosmic experience but a nettlesome obligation.

Paul's winning suggestion: First, fire up a stove and fix a hot drink. In my case, coffee, and in his, tea. But what to drink was less important than just drinking something hot. I said I thought we ought to pitch our tent first. If it had been raining or snowing, Paul likely would have agreed. But he went ahead and poured some water into the pot perched on his multifuel one-burner and broke out the instant coffee and tea bags. As soon as I was standing with a steaming mug of coffee — which smelled both beguiling and oddly homey there in the woods — I felt the wisdom of his suggestion. First, we were probably more dehydrated

*a hot drink cures all ills*

than we thought, so drinking anything was a good idea. Second, a hot drink is relaxing and brings a sense that, even in an unfamiliar and demanding wilderness setting, we were treating ourselves right. Third, making a hot drink is a comforting task, and it brings a reassuring air of decisiveness at precisely the moment when we were both worn down and faced with a whole host of steps to take in setting up a camp (check the ground, examine the surroundings for any hazards or benefits, unfurl the tent, get our gear unpacked and arranged, change clothes and shoes, sit or lie down and rest, find a latrine site, locate the nearest water — decisions, decisions, decisions).

In that first 30 minutes of identifying and settling into a campsite, many things need to get done simultaneously and precisely at the time when your energy is at lowest ebb. If you've pushed the hiking too hard and darkness is starting to encroach from the surrounding pines, it feels even more urgent to get everything done at once. Trust me on this: With a hot mug of coffee in hand, all those tasks feel much more doable and reasonable. I saw at once that Paul was onto something truly wise. Thereafter, fixing a hot drink became our first-step ritual in all backpacking trips.

## Backpacking is, to be blunt, a lot more trouble than day-hiking. Like many people, I prefer to travel light, to keep the focus on what my eyes are seeing, my ears hearing, and my memory recording. But when you're backpacking, you'll be carrying at least 20 pounds of stuff. Once you're out on a trail, especially when you've scheduled yourself to hit a particular campsite (an imperative in many popular public-land facilities), you'll have committed yourself to lifting that barge and toting that bail all day for a couple of days, regardless of how you feel or what else you want to do along the way. And if you're out for more than two nights; are carrying quantities of food, water, contingency clothes, fuel, and other hardware; and are focusing on covering distance, carrying weights, and meeting schedules, it becomes treacherously easy to start focusing wholly on your gear and forgetting why you are going to all this trouble. It begins to feel like work.

Now, having said all that, backpacking can, of course, be tremendously rewarding. It allows you to see some of the great places on Earth that you simply cannot reach and return from in a single day. And there are many such places, even in the lower 48. If you want to get out where the people are few and the nature is, well, grand, you have to backpack. The more miles you put between yourself and the nearest pavement, the fewer people you'll meet. This is particularly true in the mountainous

West, where distances are so vast that it can take you days of hiking at a vigorous pace to reach a fantastic vantage point like the high camps in Yosemite's Cathedral Range, the "Window" in the Needle Mountains southwest of Creede, Colorado, or the lookout atop Mount Wilbur in Waterton-Glacier.

First case in point: Backpacking can take you to the heights. In the Ruby Mountains of northern Nevada, a 100-mile-long north-south range with 90,000 acres of wilderness that rises up out of the sage-flat desert and an array of 10,000-foot peaks, a 40-mile trail threads along the high ridges. Tucked inside the north end of the mountains is a surprising 12-mile long, 2,000-foot-deep canyon that you can drive into (though few of the cross-country motorists droning along Interstate 80, some 20 miles to the north, sense any hint of the spectacular mountain panorama that's so close by in the Humboldt National Forest). But to take full advantage of the great views along the roof of the Ruby range, you have to backpack, allowing for a couple of days and at least one overnight.

Again, remember that hiking and backpacking are not marathon activities in which a race official is checking your time with a stopwatch in hand. Remember the rewards. Once you've reached a paradigm of a mountain peak, take a break, settle down, and give the weather and the light some time to develop. Once I hiked up to the Ruby Crest Trail and in midafternoon found an appealing wilderness site in a small hanging valley (the Rubies appear to have had an interesting time of it with the glaciers of the last ice age). It was protected from the constant wind, adjacent to some pooled-up water — one of the range's many small lakes — and surrounded by a spread of low alpine greenery. Once I was set up, I climbed up to a rim to watch the sky and the land. The wind was gusty and sharply cool and had the exhilarating clarity that comes with altitude (I was above 10,000 feet). In the hundred or so miles I could see, much of it flats broken up by other north-south mountain ranges, several local weather systems were at work, moving their whirls of clouds and curtains of shifting rain among the long slanting shafts of powerful sunlight. It was a moment to acknowledge, as a tacit recognition of the comparative importance of things, that this kind of mountain-weather spectacle unfolds all the time, whether or not you and I are there to witness it. I was looking at a lot of blue and deep bruisy purples, and silver shimmer and dark threats in the sky. In places the patchy pale green and dry-straw look of the sage flats was sunny and tranquil, as if troubled weather were only a faint memory instead of threatening from the next mountain range. Without moving, I could see rain, sun, ice, shadow, evidence of hard winds, and a gauzy back-

*bear grass*

drop that had as much to do with geology, archeology, and history as with miles of present-day space. What I could not see — with the lone exception of two partial parallel deliberate lines across the flat — was any sign whatsoever that humans had ever been anywhere in that hundred-mile radius in any direction. Except those two tracks. They were so faint in the distance and the scudding light and cloud-shadow that I had to squint to keep them in my vision. I figured that they were probably just an ad hoc ranch road tracing the passing of a pickup truck decades ago. Later I learned from a BLM ranger near Elko that I had been looking at a former stagecoach road that had, in all likelihood, also been used by Pony Express riders when they passed this way in 1860.

I went back down to my campsite to cook up and eat a dinner, then climbed back up and watched from the rim as the sun was covered by masses of turbulent streaming clouds and those clouds grew darker and darker, the night rising from all points of the compass save the west. Whoever first said night *falls?* When you're out on a mountain peak with a 360-degree view, you can plainly see the night *rising* up from the earth, the sky slowly deepening in hue as it takes on shadow from the darkened valleys, flats, and mountainsides below.

Second case in point: Once I passed a couple of days walking among the bluffs, flats, and box canyons at the west end of the Red Desert in Wyoming. It's dry and mostly flat terrain, with no real mountains to climb. But it's mysterious, too, and if you carry any curiosity about what lies up around the crook of a canyon or whether there might be some petroglyphs high on a rock wall that no one else has seen since the last fey cowboy, miner, or grumpy outlaw rigrat drilling crew jounced through here, it's a good place to wander. When you feel and enjoy that curiosity, you'll be relieved to be toting your food, water, and shelter right along with you, so you don't have to look at your watch and decide that it's time to stop and head back lest you stumble the last three miles to your parked car in total darkness. Instead, you can keep exploring right up to the time you have to eat and spread out your camp, knowing that you can start exploring again in the fresh pale light at dawn.

I was hiking along in front of my backpack, listening to my boots scuff and kick at the rocks, thinking about how utterly silent the world could be without the hummings, engines, and talk that have become our standard background white noise, when I came around a canyon buttress to face a herd of mustangs. I stopped in surprise at seeing other living animals after so much rock and sage and dust, and they — maybe ten wild ones — stood still and watched me, with only their eyes moving. They seemed less surprised than I, and clearly they had been grazing in the shadows and heard me moving toward them long before I came in sight. They looked very forthright. The alpha male, a gray-flecked stallion with a black mane and tail, stepped forward to make it clear who was in charge here, moving his head up and down slightly, the wind twisting his mane. No sounds from any of us. I took some careful steps backward, toward the straight-up wall of the canyon. I

*poppies in desert grassland*

figured they might as well see that there'd be no threats from me. I stood easily and just watched, and after a while they went back to grazing, though I could see plenty of eyes and ears turned in my direction. Unexpectedly, the horses were perfectly beautiful, lithe, and muscular under the sun, parti-colored in grays and whites and buffs and browns, and I wanted to collect them all. After a while they began to drift, grazing, on up the canyon. I let them be, grateful for the surprise meeting.

Third case in point: For my earliest adult act of deliberate camping, decades ago, I backpacked up to and along a stretch of the Appalachian Trail in south-central Pennsylvania, between U.S. 30 and the hamlet of Pine Grove Furnace. Using borrowed — and wholly ill-chosen — gear, my then-girlfriend and I made every miscalculation possible in a weekend of camping, from choosing a site after dark (we realized too late that it's not comfortable to sleep head-down on a sloping campsite) to trying to fry pancakes without a shelter in a heavy rainfall that kept diluting the batter. Still, the trail wound along a ridge that rose some 1,000 feet above the green orchards, woodlots, and pastures below the west slopes of South Mountain. I found those views of the fields below and the rows of blue-green hills and ridges undulating away to the horizon to be enchanting, evoking a longing to see and somehow embrace all the glorious country that was out there, that was real and not just imaginary. Being up there and looking down at what seemed like the whole green world changed my perspective for good; I'd just finished graduate school and had been hitting the books for years. But suddenly I saw out there the real-life setting for the history, literature, and art, for the characters, adventures, and enterprises I'd been reading about. It all looked so fresh and alive and important that I was transfixed, and very impatient to hike more trails, climb more heights, stride more mountains, and see everything out there. So I've kept at it year-round, for years.

## ON SEASONS

Unless you do most of your backpacking out in the deserts or along the drier eastern slopes of the Rockies, you'll encounter rain in any warm season. It is a fact of outdoor life. With an effective rain shell, and maybe matching pull-over rain pants, a water-shedding hat, and some dry socks to change into, rain is fairly easy to deal with.

High humidity, though, is something else. To me, it's the major discomfort factor of summer camping. It worsens the sweat factor all day as you're hiking, then makes for long sticky nights if you don't have the right gear. It can turn a too-effective sleeping bag — one rated to, say, 0°F — into an instrument of torture. Accordingly, I've always tried to plan camping trips in the East for spring or, better yet, autumn, when both the humidity and the bugs will be minimal. The comparatively lower humidity is one big reason that I prefer to backpack in the West. Even if the western summer sun is really hot, you can always cool off and dry off quickly once you stop in some shade.

Summer is the preferred backpacking season for most people for a handful of reasons: The kids are out of school. It's generally warm enough that you need pack only a minimal load of clothing. And it's the only time you can backpack in upper elevations in many of the western mountains, in places like Rocky Mountain National Park or Waterton-Glacier or in many parts of the Sierra Nevada, because July and August are about the only times the snow is out of the passes, allowing you to hike or climb to the top.

In the spring and early summer, backpacking offers other rewards. Chances are you won't encounter the prime-time trail traffic of mid-summer, wildlife is more plentiful and active, and in places the wild-flowers will bring great color to your traverse. True, the weather is less predictable and demands a wider range of clothes and other gear; during a single day of hiking in northern New Mexico in April, my wife and I once experienced every kind of weather except for tornadoes: sun, clouds, wind, rain, sleet, hail, snow, and even a blinding dust storm.

Autumn is, for many experienced backpackers, the best time of all. It can be warm during the day and blessedly cool (and maybe without the humidity) at night. If the area has already had a cold night, the insects will have gone to ground. If it's early fall and you're hiking in a deciduous forest, the colors can be overwhelming. Later in the season when the leaves are mostly down, you can see farther through the forest and, from ridge-top trails, enjoy far more expansive views. Birds are migrating and other wildlife may be active. (But a cautionary note: Deer, elk, and moose are in reproduction mode and the males may be pretty touchy; don't approach anything with antlers. And as you get into later fall, check for the dates of local hunting seasons. When it is deer, elk, or bear season, steer clear of the woods and wilderness areas no matter how much blaze-orange clothing you wear. Bullets carry, and accidents do happen.)

Winter camping can be done and can even be fun, but it demands more attention to balancing the work-versus-fun equation than does camping in other seasons. Winter camping also takes more planning, more forethought, more energy, and generally more and heavier-duty gear than is needed in spring, summer, or autumn. This is especially true if you anticipate camping in a region where there is substantial snow on the ground (or likely to fall on you). Then matters of comfort and safety become even more important and demand more planning. But if there are places you must get to and see in deep winter, whether on boots, on snowshoes, or on cross-country skis, you can camp in relative comfort. I have actually slept soundly in a tent through nights when the outside temperature was below -25°F, but it took some doing. And of course winter camping is rewarding: You won't encounter any crowds, and you may see the world in a way that few people ever see it, with the freshest of snows marked only by the tracks of the hares and other animals that have been out and about under those star-bright winter skies.

Some cautionary notes for winter camping:

**Planning.** Lower your sights when it comes to time and distance. If you are mushing through the snow, on foot or skis or snowshoes, you won't cover the mileage you could on a bare trail. Everything you do — from fixing a snack to defecating — takes much longer in the snow and cold. Also, in the northern half of the country in full winter, the light fails around four o'clock, so plan your camping accordingly.

**Gear.** Use real winter gear, and mind the temperature ratings and dampness characteristics of your clothes, your boots, and your sleeping bag (see the following discussion).

**Boots.** Depending on how you are getting around, appropriate boots are essential for keeping snow out and your feet dry and warm. They should be insulated, be at least eight inches high, and have some kind of closure or collar for a snug fit above your ankle.

**Practice.** Practice performing every camping act, from taking out a water bottle to rigging your tent, in darkness and with gloves and coat on. It's useful to learn in advance that some zippers jam and some things don't unscrew, unfasten, yield to a knife, switch on and off, or stay put when you are fumbling at them with thick wool gloves covering your fingers. You may want to change the way you stow your tent or pack your backpack to ease and simplify your winter operation.

**Stove.** Check ahead of time that your stove will function efficiently in very low temperatures and windy conditions. A dark and stormy night at 9,000 feet on a snow-smothered Colorado mountain is not the occasion to discover that you cannot heat up a mug of soup.

**Cautions.** All the hiking rules of navigation, pacing yourself, keeping an eye on potential hazards on the trail, and monitoring your condition are doubly important in the snow and cold.

**Waterproofing.** Above all, do whatever is necessary to stay dry from head to toe.

**Glare protection.** Don't forget sunglasses and sunblock cream.

## GEAR

When backpacking, the selection and use of gear is more critical to comfort than when day-hiking. In general, lighter is better, simply because it reduces the poundage that you are expending your own personal calories to carry. (While you're calculating weights of gear and trying to lighten everything, think about losing some weight yourself; it might be more cost-effective to shed ounces from your body than from the gear you buy.) But lightness does not outweigh all other criteria. Some superlight gear won't stand up to truly atrocious weather or to rough handling and may not last the many years that most camping gear is good for. Also, a cost-versus-diminishing-returns curve is in effect here: Below a certain weight threshold for all the major gear — jackets, packs, tents, sleeping bag — lighter and lighter gear costs more and more money.

First, the backpack itself: For a time, the big decision was whether to use an external- or internal-frame pack. But external-frame packs are now fairly rare, and internal-frame packs are much improved, lighter, and more comfortable than they used to be. These packs are shaped and stabilized by semirigid stays of aircraft-quality aluminum or carbon-fiber. The more important considerations are volume, "suspension systems" (that is, the various straps, belts, pads, and harnesses that fasten the whole pack to your back), adjustability, pockets and access, arrangement of attachment points, and even materials. Volume is usually noted in cubic inches, and for two- to four-night camping jaunts, a backpack in the range of 3,500 to 5,000 cubic inches is about right. Look for a pack at the lower end of that range that weighs six pounds or less.

When selecting a backpack, it is possible to make some decisions by eyeballing a catalog or website photographs and reading the specifications — which material, the color (bright colors are, alas, not much in fashion these days), and the number, size, and arrangement of pockets

*a multi-pocket pack*

and attachment points. But the fit of the pack on your individual back is the most important factor, and to determine fit, you must try a pack on. Then check all the ways to adjust the load, as the more flexibility a pack has in adjustments, the better your odds of finding a combination that allows you to carry the requisite 25 to 40 pounds of stuff — comfortably. The number and arrangement of pockets is important to lower the aggravation quotient when you're hiking under difficult conditions and have to access a water bottle, a map, a compass, a snack, or a change of clothes at frequent intervals. Some of the packs designed for mountain climbers have minimal outside pockets — minimal outside everything, in fact, to minimize the chances of snagging some part of the pack on some part of the mountain at a decisive moment during a climb. If a smooth exterior is not a necessity, go for the backpacks with several easy-access pockets. Manufacturers' web sites offer a lot of good information. But there is no substitute for going to an outdoor-gear store and comparing an assortment of backpacks.

Tents are good for repelling wind, rain, snow, and some of the chilliness of the night. And they're good for separating you from the resident mosquitoes, flies, scorpions, and snakes. Still, a tent is not totally essential if you're camping in benign weather and in a place that's fairly bug-free. Then you could get by with only a light tarpaulin or fly.

Tents are available in a very confusing variety of shapes, sizes, colors, options, weights, and materials. And prices, of course. Again, a useful amount of information is available in catalogs and on manufacturers' and some retailers' web sites.

The major decision is how many adults are likely to be sleeping in the tent. Once that is decided, consider these factors: Select a size and shape that permits two grown-ups to sit up simultaneously and maybe pull on some clothes at the same time without feeling like two pieces of a jigsaw puzzle. Or like Siamese twins. Bad weather may occasionally compel you to spend some hours in your tent, reading or playing cards or fixing a meal, and that is no fun when you can't sit up comfortably. For two or three people, a comfortable tent size is in the range of 35 to 40 square feet, at a weight of 7 to 9 pounds.

*erecting the tent*

Most tents are made of ripstop polyester or nylon and come complete with poles, fly, stuff sack, instructions, and patch kit. Look for one that has a fly for extra weather protection and other uses, as well as some form of "window" on more than one side. A window is not just a matter of sightseeing; it's also a matter of safety and psychic comfort. I've been camping with more than one adult who suffers from "tent claustrophobia" and, despite otherwise unquestionable physical courage, cannot stand the feeling of blind isolation in a tent, the sense that dangerous beings could be lurking in the wide world that's just outside the tent wall but that cannot be seen.

Select a tent that can be simply and quickly unpacked and packed, assembled and disassembled, even in darkness and in rain, without your having to read several pages of challenging instructions. And practice putting it up and taking it down a couple of times before you take it on its first camping trip. The idea, remember, is to put yourself in a position of enjoying rare sights and sounds, not to put yourself in a position of slavery to your gear.

One other consideration: If you plan to camp in snow, in sand, or on bare rock above tree line, look for a free-standing tent design, that is, one that's not dependent on tent pegs to define and hold its shape. I learned the hard way that pegs won't hold in loose sand and, therefore, the tent won't stay up.

And, of course, never cook or use an open flame inside a tent. Tents are almost always nylon or polyester, both highly flammable materials.

A sleeping bag can keep you warm, but the sleeping pad makes you comfortable. The worst sleepless night I ever endured on a camping trip happened because I had a too-thin foam pad that I neglected to try out before hiking. I'd borrowed it for a night of unplanned camping in New Mexico, and it was simply not dense enough to cushion me from sticks, pebbles, and irregularities on the ground. I was warm enough, but miserable and sleepless, because it was simply impossible to get comfortable. So, whether you're getting an inflatable or a dense foam sleeping pad, make certain it actually will cushion and insulate you. It's really the only thing that keeps you from sleeping on the cold hard ground.

Sleeping bags work by creating dead air spaces with either natural goose down or some kind of manufactured filler. Bags are rated for the minimum ambient temperature at which they are generally effective — rated good to +15°F, for instance — but I would add a generous margin for contingencies and if camping in cool or cold weather would choose a bag rated to 0°F. For midsummer nights, such a bag would be too warm and sticky, but in all other seasons, it will give a good margin of comfort. If you plan to do a lot of camping in warm sticky weather, get a lightweight bag lined with a soft cloth, such as brushed polyester, which feels like cotton flannel but dries more rapidly.

Down works better for lower temperatures, but it can absorb and hold moisture; if a goose-down bag gets wet, it is slow to dry and loses its effectiveness. A bag made with Polarguard or Fiberfill needs more fill than a down-filled bag offering the same insulation value and therefore generally weighs more and compresses less readily. However, a manufactured-fill bag has the advantages of not taking on moisture and drying more rapidly. So it's a better choice if you're not shaving weight by the quarter-ounce and expect to encounter dampness. As with other kinds of camping gear, lighter is better but more expensive for sleeping bags. A good compromise might be a Polarguard- or Hollofill-insulated bag that's good to +15°F, weighs four pounds or less, and rolls to a stuffed size of about 9 inches by 18 inches. Look for such helpful touches as a drawstring collar, a pillow bag, and baffled construction that keeps the insulation evenly distributed to avoid cold spots.

Shape and fit are also important in a sleeping bag. To be effective, a sleeping bag can't be too big or your body can't generate enough of a warm-air layer to keep you cozy; if a bag is too small and tight, you'll be too constricted to sleep comfortably.

Beyond those major pieces of equipment, there are a few other items to consider packing for an overnight stay (above and beyond what I've already suggested for day hikes):

**A headlamp-style flashlight.** You may look like a lost miner, but having light shining on what you're looking at — and still having both hands free — can be a great advantage.

**Tarp.** Carry a tarp that is, say, 8 feet square, or a lightweight aluminized space blanket for an emergency fly or tent shelter, an extra wrap, an extra ground cloth, and — especially in winter — a surface on which

*headlamp-style light*

to place cooking gear and food; it is much too easy to lose small essential items, like a knife, in soft snow.

**Plastic bags.** You'll need plastic bags with zip-seal tops to carry all your food going in and for packing waste back out.

**Stuff sacks.** Small nylon stuff sacks in assorted sizes and colors with drawstring closures can help you organize everything in your pack.

*braided nylon rope*

**Rope.** About 25 feet of lightweight braided nylon rope is very useful for a great variety of camp services, from hanging clothes for drying to securing your tent. If you're heading into bear country, you'll need extra rope for hoisting a food bag out of reach.

## DRESSING FOR BACKPACKING

All the truths about hiking clothes also apply to backpacking clothes, with only a few alterations. Boots should be sturdier. When toting along an extra 20 to 40 pounds, the stresses on your feet — and the consequences of a misstep and a turned ankle — are magnified. Often you can get away with light running shoes or cross-trainers for day-hiking, but more substantial boots with heavy-duty soles and real ankle support are a must for multiday backpacking. The boots should be water-repellent; if you step in a creek and wet a boot, it's not as though you'll be back at the car in a couple of hours. Some of us like to change shoes frequently; I generally devote some of those precious cubic inches in my backpack to alternate footwear, such as a pair of leather boat shoes. They're a welcome change in the campsite at the end of a day of slogging along in heavy hiking boots.

Spare socks and underwear are imperative on a camping trip. Beyond these basic items, think *layers.* It's tempting to start packing a change of clothing for every day, the way you might if you were taking a vacation trip to Tuscany and intending to stay in a hotel and dine in a different trattoria every evening. But on the trail, nobody cares if you look a little grubby and monotonous, as long as you are comfortable. So go for the loose-cut trousers and several lightweight layers that you can put on or take off to adjust for morning chill, noonday sun, afternoon wind, and possible rain showers. And if you are backpacking in a cool season, include warmer layers, in wool, poly fleece, wind-stopping Gore-tex nylon, or even down- or Fiberfill-lined jackets. Try out all layers of outerwear with your backpack on and adjusted to the added bulk — ahead of time. And bring a warm hat and gloves even if you don't think you need them.

## ON FOOD AND COOKING

Before heading up from Grand Lake, Colorado, to a three-night jaunt along a wilderness trail in Rocky Mountain National Park as part of a lengthy writing assignment from National Geographic, my wife and I shopped for camp food. While she was rounding up the usual containers of ramen noodles, dried soup mixes, pasta, cheese, instant coffee, and powdered milk, I went in search of oranges and apples and along the way noticed some fresh strawberries. What the hell, I thought. I bought the strawberries and a small box of half-and-half, which I planned to decant into a pre-cooled insulated container. The weather was cool enough that the cream would be okay, and I could carry the strawberries in a plastic box. I planned to surprise my wife with some strawberries and cream for breakfast.

It worked. The next morning, at our first wilderness area site deep in a rugged fir thicket at about 8,000 feet, after we'd gotten the coffee underway, I broke out the surprise. Strawberries and cream! She couldn't get over it. "How'd you do that, Michael?" she kept asking. My response was that despite the fact that this was wilderness camping, they weren't paying us to suffer. Why not treat us to fresh breakfast on the first morning of the trip? The point is that backpacking food does not always have to be dehydrated material that feels and tastes like insulation. Carry some perishables for the first day and fresh fruits that are on the heavy side, like oranges, and eat them first. Save the drier and lighter foods for later in the trip.

When it comes to camp cooking and eating, planning really helps — a fact that even I, a lifelong planningphobe, will admit. To strike that balance between carrying enough of the right foods and fluids and not carrying too much weight, you must plan. First, about water: You'll need two to three quarts of water per person per day, and more for food prep and cleanup, and even more if it's winter or if you're headed for the desert or for high elevations. That's a lot of water and weight to carry. But unless you're going to true desert where there will not be any potable water available, you won't have to pack it all in. Figure on treating the local water by boiling, filtering, purification (latter two mean buying and using some hardware), or using iodine or chlorine. There was a time in living memory when you could safely drink stream water in wilderness areas or high-altitude places where no sheep had been grazing, but those days are over. Sadly, there are very few unpolluted streams left in the lower 48, and it's pointless to take a chance. So carry a couple of quart-size Nalgene bottles of fresh water, and prepare to boil or treat the rest of what you'll need.

To save on fuel, figure on cooking only one meal a day — dinner. Otherwise, eat foods that need no heating or other complex preparations. Dry cereals (like granola) with powdered milk are good, as are hearty multigrain breads. I never carry regular sandwich bread; it's too soft and bulky and doesn't give you much caloric value. Instead, bring flat breads like pita and tortillas or dense bread products like bagels and English muffins. Dried fruits like raisins, apricots, or apples are also easy to transport. Coffee is the big exception to the no-cook rule for me; it's simply a necessity for getting my day and my heart going. So while I am happy with cold granola for breakfast, I still crank up the Coleman

*local water must be purified for drinking*

for coffee water. For lunch and periodically during the day I might have a dense cheese like Colby cheddar, Monterey Jack, or fontina (they'll easily stand going unrefrigerated for four days if kept in plastic wrap) and maybe a hard salami and some lightweight water-bearing vegetables like raw carrots or celery. And gorp (trail mix), of course.

I prefer to eat often during a long hike. The breaks are good for a stop and look-around, and some of us really feel the energy flag when it's been more than two hours since the last snack. For one thing, you burn up about twice as many calories during a serious hike as you do during a routine workday. Once when my friend Paul and I were pushing hard on a long uphill stretch in the mountains in Glacier, on our way to a destination that he really wanted to photograph, I could tell when I needed to eat not by any stomach pangs but by a leaden feeling of simply running low on energy. "Out of gas!" we'd exclaim, and shed our packs for some chow time. We'd drink our brought-along water, mixed with lemonade powder and sugar, and soon be ready for some more steady climbing.

All the foods carried on a backpacking trip, except for items like dehydrated soups that come packed in paper or plastic envelopes, should be removed from their bottles, cans, or boxes and repacked in

*lightweight camping stove*

small plastic bags (doubled against breakage and leaks). Commercial packaging is surprisingly heavy and bulky and should be dispensed with before you take one step wearing a backpack.

Now about dinner: You'll need to cook, and this means packing along a stove and fuel (no open fires, please, except in life-and-death emergency situations; the risks are just too great). There's a whole panoply of types, styles, and weights of camping stoves, and some backpackers can get downright emotional about the rightness of their choices. The "lightness at any cost" school favors the extremely light mountaineering specials. I prefer to pay the weight penalty and go with the old traditional Model-T technology: the Coleman Peak One or equivalent one-burner that runs on Coleman fuel (which should always be carried in a good-quality, tight-sealing aluminum fuel bottle). During one winter camping venture into the Wind River range in western Wyoming, when a group of six of us skied our way up through some very stormy conditions and deep cold, I was ragged mercilessly by my mountaineering compadres about carting that heavy Coleman. They referred to it as "Mike's kitchen range" and "Mike's cinder-block stove." However, on that first morning at about 8,400 feet, when we came flapping and staggering out of our snow-banked tents, guess whose teeny alcohol stoves couldn't work up enough BTUs to boil water? And guess who got very popular as he cranked out mug after mug of steaming cocoa and coffee?

Bear in mind that cleaning up in the wild is far more difficult and messy than cooking, so keep the cooking simple and clean. Work mostly with water and don't fry anything — unless you're on a fishing trip and land a meal-sized trout. And work with versatile, lightweight foods like rice or pasta. Any variety can be boiled, and for additional flavors and nourishment you can add to these basics any number of other ingredients: cheese, canned tuna (carried in a strong plastic bag and used in the first day), red sauce, sun-dried tomatoes or other dried vegetables, preserved red meat like hard salami, and mushrooms, either fresh or dried. One of my favorite moves is to carry a couple of envelopes of dehydrated vegetable soup and pour some of the ingredients in with the boiling pasta or rice, for variety of taste.

Also pack along some dried spices, such as oregano, pepper, dill, thyme, rosemary, and even curry. They weigh practically nothing, and when used for a dinner main dish, they can make the difference between just dutifully shoveling down fuel or enjoying a wilderness dining experience.

A good friend and colleague, naturalist/author Bruce Stutz, is a whiz at finding and identifying safe edible mushrooms in the wild. So he has a great advantage at dinner time on a backpacking trip. He always seems to locate tasty morels. Of course, if you cannot distinguish between good and bad mushrooms — beyond any doubt — don't go there. Lest you end up turning green like Babar's father. Some wild ingredients can be found and added to your meal safely, depending on where you are. I've enhanced camp meals with sage and pinole nuts in New Mexico and with wild scallions in many places. Just make sure you can positively identify anything you put in the cookpot.

Always bring chocolate for dessert. And an assortment of teabags.

To cook, you'll need a good 1½- or 2-quart aluminum pot with a lid. A pot with a removable handle will facilitate packing. Beyond that, you need only a flat aluminum pan or fry pan — again with a removable handle — that can double as a dinner dish. Plus a mug for hot or cold liquids and a bowl and a spoon to eat with — all in cheap, tough, lightweight plastic. One larger spoon to stir and serve with is useful. These few items — along with that Swiss Army knife that never leaves your side — are all you need. Most campers carry too much cookware. It's shiny and tempting in the store but a weight and a bother to clean on the trail. For cleanup, bring some quart-sized zip-seal plastic bags, a couple of rags, environmentally safe detergent, and a Scotch-brite pad.

After dinner and cleanup, retire early and drift off, listening to the night sounds. That way, you'll get a good long sleep and still be able to get up early. Do yourself a favor and get up and out at first light. Wildlife, including the birds, will be stirring, and you may be rewarded for your early start by seeing some critters you would never otherwise see. And, coffee in hand, you'll get to witness a sunrise in a wild setting where few other people are present and see the world the way it really is, the way it has been every other morning while you were back in the city cursing the alarm clock. That's why you backpacked out there, isn't it?

# Great American Hikes

—

I have hiked high and low, in all kinds of terrain, far and wide across the lower 48 states and Hawaii, and I do have favorite hikes — places that are always among the most rewarding of wild and scenic trails. Of course I have not hiked on every great trail in every state, but what follows is a checklist of the ones I have enjoyed the most. It only scratches the surface, and I am aware of the large omissions, but these are the places I would return to in a heartbeat.

There are hundreds, if not thousands, of good trails in nearly every state in the union, distributed through hundreds of national parks and monuments and wildlife sanctuaries, and probably even more trails in the thousands of state parks and recreation areas.

## NATIONAL PARKS

Our great national parks and monuments (376 of them at last count) offer an incredible array of diversions from swimming to spelunking, but the ones with the largest number and variety of pure hiking venues, in my opinion, are listed below (from east to west, roughly).

For detailed information on hiking trails, maps, directions, seasons, and hours, consult the main National Park Service web site — www.nps.gov — and branch out from there.

**Acadia National Park, Bar Harbor, Maine.** Located on Mount Desert Island. Phone 207-288-3338

**Cape Cod National Seashore, Wellfleet, Massachusetts.** Encompasses a long stretch of the outer Cape. Phone 508-255-3421

**Delaware Water Gap National Recreation Area, Bushkill, Pennsylvania.** Sits on the Delaware River. Phone 570-588-2451

**Assateague Island National Seashore, Berlin, Maryland.** Long stretches of Atlantic barrier island beach: broad, flat, windswept — and the farther you hike, the more solitary it gets. Phone 410-641-1441

**Catoctin Mountain Park, Thurmont, Maryland.** Great hikes in the mountains of western Maryland. Phone 301-663-9388

**Chesapeake and Ohio Canal National Historical Park, Sharpsburg, Maryland.** Along the Potomac River between Maryland and Virginia/West Virginia. Phone 301-739-4200

**Shenandoah National Park, Luray, Virginia.** Offers a wide range of hikes in the Blue Ridge Mountains/Skyline Drive. Phone 540-999-3500

**Blue Ridge Parkway, Asheville, North Carolina.** Over 450 miles of parkway along the Blue Ridge Mountains, in the southern Appalachian highlands. Phone 828-298-0398

**Great Smoky Mountains National Park, Gatlinburg, Tennessee.** Over 500,000 acres of forest; a World Heritage site. Phone 865-436-1200

**Pictured Rocks National Lakeshore, Munising, Michigan.** 40 miles of cliffs and beaches along the forested shore of Lake Superior, in the Upper Peninsula. Phone 906-387-3700

**Big Bend National Park, Texas.** Over 800,000 acres of desert and forested mountains along the Rio Grande. This place is so big it has its own zip code: 79834. Phone 915-477-2251

**Hovenweep National Monument, Cortez, Colorado.** Anasazi ruins and sagebrush in the loneliest place in North America. Phone 970-562-4282

**Rocky Mountain National Park, Estes Park, Colorado.** The name says it all: great mountain hiking on both sides of the Divide. Phone 970-586-1206

**Grand Teton National Park, Moose, Wyoming.** Great snow-topped peaks plus flats teeming with elk; near Jackson Hole. Phone 307-739-3300

**Yellowstone National Park, Yellowstone NP, Wyoming.** The oldest and wildest park, offering everything from geysers to grizzlies, with over 2 million acres of forest, mountain, river, and lake. Phone 307-344-7381

**Glacier National Park, West Glacier, Montana.** Real glaciers and stunning mountains in a million acres of wilderness life. Phone 406-888-7800

**Arches National Park, Moab, Utah.** One of a handful of incredibly colorful rocky parks in Utah. Phone 435-719-2299

**Bryce Canyon National Park, Bryce Canyon, Utah.** More red-rock, more erosion, more forests, great views. Phone 435-834-5322

**Canyonlands National Park, Moab, Utah.** River canyons and petroglyphs in three separate zones southwest of Moab. Phone 435-719-2313

**Zion National Park, Springdale, Utah.** Over 200 square miles of arches, eroded canyons, mesas, and cliffs — wild and remote — south of Cedar City. Phone 435-772-3256

**Grand Canyon National Park, Grand Canyon, Arizona.** The great mile-deep erosive achievement of the Colorado River; unmatched scenery and deceptively rough trails. Phone 928-638-7888

**Chaco Culture National Historical Park, Nageezi, New Mexico.** The Anasazi ruins are the thing, but mesa and desert canyon trails hold many surprises. Phone 505-786-7014

**El Malpais National Monument, Grants, New Mexico.** Black volcanic lava flows created one of the weirdest "badlands" 'scapes on the continent. Phone 505-783-4774

**Gila Cliff Dwellings National Monument, Silver City, New Mexico.** Smallish thirteenth-century cliffhouses are surrounded by a high, dry, empty forest wilderness. Phone 505-536-9461

**North Cascades National Park, Sedro-Woolley, Washington.** Wild and scenic; wet/dry mountains, glaciers, and demanding trails in almost 700,000 acres. Phone 360-856-5700

**Mount Rainier National Park, Ashford, Washington.** 250,000 acres of forest wilderness centered on 14,410-foot volcanic Rainier. Phone 360-569-2211

**Olympic National Park, Port Angeles, Washington.** An isolated, unique wilderness with rain forests and mountain glaciers along the Pacific coast. Phone 360-565-3130

**Joshua Tree National Park, Twentynine Palms, California.** Unique trees in a serious desert setting; bring water. Phone 760-367-5500

**Kings Canyon/Sequoia National Park, Three Rivers, California.** Big Trees by the grove, a powerful river, and a west-slope entry into the High Sierra. Phone 559-565-3341

**Point Reyes National Seashore, Point Reyes Station, California.** Great beaches, tidepools, and sea lions at the ancestral home of Fog. Phone 415-464-5100

**Yosemite National Park, Yosemite, California.** Mind-boggling concentration of soaring cliffs, spectral falls, and vast views, with strenuous mountain hiking. Phone 209-372-0200

*wildflowers*

# OTHER PUBLIC LANDS

Outside the national parks, there are many, many excellent hiking venues. Strong possibilities include the National Forest and Bureau of Land Management (BLM) lands and the state parks and forests that are close to the national parks and share the same topography, weather, and types of forests or grasslands. Often those places differ from adjacent national parks only in having far fewer visitors.

Among those different types of public lands and wildlife reservations, I have especially enjoyed hiking in certain areas, noted below. These are my favorites (again in roughly east-to-west order), with no pretense of universal, "all-states" coverage. And remember: All other factors being equal, I favor places with high-altitude long views.

## IN THE EAST

**Mount Greylock State Reservation, Lanesborough, Massachusetts.** A thickly forested park centered on the state's highest (3,491 feet) peak. It's laced with 60 miles of trails, including a long stretch of the Appalachian Trail, and topped by a rustic campers' lodge with wonderful views of several states.

**Green Mountain National Forest, Rutland, Vermont.** Most of the southwest corner of Vermont lies in this 350,000-acre mountain/forest area. Best known for its ski developments, it's a rewarding hiking venue, with five wilderness areas and over 500 miles of roller-coaster trails, including stretches of the Appalachian Trail and the Long Trail.

**Camel's Hump State Park, Essex Junction, Vermont.** With a summit above 4,000 feet, any climb here will take you up through several biozones. It's damp; a lot of rain falls on these hardwood forests. It's traversed by the Long Trail.

**White Mountain National Forest, Laconia, New Hampshire.** Over a thousand miles of well-developed and maintained hiking trails crisscross the Presidential Mountains in north-central New Hampshire. Among the most scenic areas: Franconia Notch State Park and the trails on 4,000-foot Cannon Mountain. Weather can be dicey in any season.

**Adirondack Mountain Park, New York.** This park is huge, larger than most national parks and some states, occupying most of upstate New York between Lake Champlain and Lake Ontario. The best hiking areas are the Cranberry Lake region in the northwest and the High Peaks mountain wilderness zone near Saranac Lakes — but there are over 2,000 miles of trails to explore here.

**Catskill Mountain Park, New York.** This park occupies another huge area of New York's mountains and forests, and it's crisscrossed with trails. Among the good hiking areas are the Devil's Path, the approaches to Slide Mountain, and other trails in the Neversink watershed.

**Harriman/Bear Mountain State Parks, Orange and Rockland Counties, New York.** About 80 square miles of hilly wooded terrain adjacent to the Hudson River, with 200 miles of hiking trails. Plenty of loop trails. Easy access from population centers.

**Hudson Highland State Park, Cold Spring, New York.** This one is right on the Hudson River, with steep rocky trails jumping directly up from water level. Definitely worth the climbs for the unique, stunning views of the narrowest part of the lower Hudson Valley.

**Minnewaska State Park, New York.** West of New Paltz, in the Shawangunk Mountain range, and famed among rock climbers as the "Gunks." It's a rugged ridgeline of quartz conglomerate outcrops with terrific views.

**Stokes State Forest/High Point State Park, northwest of Sussex, New Jersey.** Contiguous areas containing some 20 miles of the Appalachian Trail atop Kittatinny Mountain, as well as other shorter trails in a mountain setting near the Delaware River.

**Roosevelt State Park, Pennsylvania.** This park encompasses 60 miles of the Delaware Canal, offering a broad, easy towpath along the Delaware River between Easton and Morrisville. A linear hiking experience among stone cottages, locks, bridges, and other engineering artifacts from the century of canal boating (1830–1930).

**Ricketts Glen State Park, Benton, Pennsylvania.** Uncrowded large remote park with virgin stands of hemlock and trails that loop down into gorges, alongside dozens of waterfalls. Similar terrain in adjacent state game lands.

**Hickory Run State Park, White Haven, Pennsylvania.** Surprisingly (it's right on Interstate 80) undeveloped large park with comfortable loop trails among white pine forest. Also includes a peculiar boulder field left behind by the Wisconsin Glacier some 18,000 years ago.

**Michaux State Forest, Fayetteville, Pennsylvania.** A classic northeastern ridge-and-valley setting of some 80,000 acres that includes 36 miles of Appalachian Trail along South Mountain, with many side access trails. Includes Pine Grove Furnace State Park.

**Hawk Mountain Sanctuary, Kempton, Pennsylvania.** On the Blue Ridge just south of the Appalachian Trail, offering high clear views of migrating raptors in the spring and fall. Trails lead up to two lookouts that are among the best birdwatching sites on the continent.

**Buchanan State Forest, McConnellsburg, Pennsylvania.** Scenic Tuscarora Mountains (elevations near 2,800 feet) and gorges, with many forest trails, wild and scenic areas, and dramatic overlooks. Includes Cowans Gap State Park and abuts many large state game lands.

**Blue Knob State Park, Imler, Pennsylvania.** In the heart of the Appalachians and best known for its namesake ski area (3,100-foot elevation), this area has a challenging trail system with many overlooks.

**Cunningham Falls State Park, Thurmont, Maryland.** Adjacent to Catoctin Mountain Park (which is administered by the National Park Service because it contains the presidential retreat at Camp David), this is a trail-laced stretch of classic Appalachian mountain scenery with thick stands of hardwoods, fresh streams, and views of adjacent valleys. Another old iron-furnace site.

**South Mountain State Park, Jefferson, Maryland.** A long quartzite ridge that includes 40 miles of Appalachian Trail from Harpers Ferry, West Virginia, to the Pennsylvania line, with side trails, numerous overlooks, and other state parks and historic sites along the way. Mellow and scenic.

**George Washington National Forest, Harrisonburg, Virginia.** Over a million acres of woodlands sprawling in three sections along the Allegheny Mountains (peaks over 4,400 feet) on the west side of the Shenandoah Valley. Includes 70 miles of the Appalachian Trail plus hundreds of miles of other trails; much of it is underutilized compared with Shenandoah/Blue Ridge Park system. The most scenic hiking areas are around Massanutten Mountain south of Front Royal and the Sherando Lake area south of Charlottesville.

**Watoga State Forest, Marlinton, West Virginia.** In a remote setting of Appalachian coves and rugged ridges, a deeply forested park with over 40 miles of hiking trails amidst thick azalea and rhododendron. Adjacent to vast Monongahela National Forest.

**Lake Superior State Forest, Michigan.** Trails throughout; non-motorized trails are referred to as "pathways." This is not the only great hiking opportunity in Michigan. As a whole, the entire upper peninsula (the "U.P.") is nearly all national or state forest, a vast stretch of second-growth pine and dark rivers.

**Beaverhead National Forest, Red Rock Lakes National Wildlife Refuge, Lakeview, Montana.** Open trails at the 7,000-foot level atop the ridgeline south of the lakes afford easy hiking with great views into Montana's Gravelly Range. Very lightly used.

**Bitterroot National Forest, Hamilton, Montana.** Along the impassably rugged peaks of the Bitterroot Range, the Continental Divide forms the Montana/Idaho border. Numerous trails lead up into this high country. In fact, much of western Montana is national forest and offers great wild and scenic hiking.

**Lewis & Clark and Flathead National Forests, Montana.** South of Glacier National Park, a vast stretch of the Rocky Mountains lies within the Lewis & Clark and Flathead National Forests. Within those forests are the Great Bear (this is grizzly country), the Scapegoat, and the Bob Marshall Wilderness areas. This is rough, wild country, with mountain peaks at 9,000 feet and above.

**The Bridger-Teton National Forest, Pinedale, Wyoming.** Southeast of Yellowstone, the Wind River Range offers classic snow-peaked mountains (half a dozen of them topping 13,000 feet), with many lakes, alpine vistas, and true wilderness hiking on miles of great trails. One of the best mountain-hiking venues in North America.

**The Red Desert or Great Divide Basin, Rock Springs, Wyoming.** 100 miles of hot, dry, and largely empty desert, with badland hills around its perimeter. Not a wilderness and once the site of oil and gas production (some areas are still littered with old rigs) and uranium mining, it's a unique landscape with many more mustangs than hikers.

**The San Juan Mountains, Creede, Colorado.** A long bight of Continental Divide mountains (many peaks above tree line and above 12,000 feet) encircles the old mining town of Creede, and the Rio Grande National Forest between Del Norte and Silverton includes numerous primitive and wilderness areas and more miles of great trails than you could hike in a lifetime.

**The Gunnison National Forest, Gunnison, Colorado.** Some of the best ski areas in the West are located here, but during the warm weather, there's high-country hiking in the mountains between Route 50 and Route 82.

**The Rocky Mountains, Colorado.** In the front range of the Rockies west of Denver, it's possible to hike trails and old mountain roads from one old mining town to another: Idaho Springs, Central City, Empire, Silver Plume, and more.

**Santa Fe, New Mexico.** Santa Fe is surrounded by worthy hiking venues, with numerous pueblos, Anasazi ruins (in Bandelier National Monument), and wilderness areas in the Sangre de Cristo Mountains. Cosmic country with incredible scenery and weather.

**Santa Fe and Carson National Forests, Santa Fe and Taos, New Mexico.** Northwest of Santa Fe in the Abiquiu/Ghost Ranch country (and adjacent Pueblo and Apache reservations), there's high desert mesas in colors that must be seen to be believed. Plus utter silence and solitude.

**Gila National Forest, Silver City, New Mexico.** Several mountain ranges (Black Range, Mogollon Mountains, Mimbres Mountains, San Francisco Mountains), mostly covered by mature stands of ponderosa, and numerous wilderness and primitive areas make up some of the driest, emptiest hiking country in the Southwest. You'll be on your own here. And it feels haunted.

**Monument Valley Navajo Tribal Park, Kayenta, Arizona.** If you've seen the classic Westerns (Stagecoach, She Wore a Yellow Ribbon, The Searchers, My Darling Clementine), then you've seen this one many times. All those mittenlike red sandstone buttes and rocky spires and the unearthly colors. The scale is so large that most people drive it, but you can hike.

**Humboldt-Toiyabe National Forest, Sparks, Nevada.** The Ruby Mountains, rising thousands of feet above the Nevada desert, encompass a vast deep canyon and a long stretch of unpopulated, above-tree-line trails offering some of the longest and most stunning mountain views in the West. A long way from almost everywhere, but worth the trip.

**Sequoia National Forest, Porterville, California.** The forest includes sections of the Pacific Crest Trail, the National Scenic Trail that follows the top of the Sierra Nevada. Sections of this high mountain trail afford knife-edge views back toward the Central Valley and eastward over the deep rosy deserts.

## MAJOR ESTABLISHED SUPPLIERS
## OF HIKING AND BACKPACKING EQUIPMENT

This is not a complete list, nor is it a set of recommendations based on testing of every item. I have used gear from many of these manufacturers, with at least satisfactory results. Most reputable retailers of outdoor sports gear carry products from these manufacturers, or you can contact them directly for product information. Nearly all maintain useful and informative web sites.

**The Coleman Company, Inc., Wichita, KS**
Phone: 800-835-3278
Web site: coleman.com
*Packs, tents, sleeping bags, clothing, footwear, cooking gear, lighting.*

**Dana Design, Vashon, WA**
Phone: 888-357-3262
Web site: danadesign.com
*Packs and tents.*

**Eureka Camping Tents, Binghamton, NY**
Phone: 800-572-8822
Web site:
  eurekacamping.com
*Tents.*

**Gregory Mountain Products, Temecula, CA**
Phone: 800-477-3420
Web site: gregorypacks.com
*Packs, travel gear.*

**Jansport, Appleton, WI**
Phone: 800-346-8239
Web site: jansport.com
*Packs and travel gear.*

**Kelty Products, Boulder, CO**
Phone: 800-423-2320
Web site: kelty.com
*Packs, tents, sleeping bags, travel gear, children's gear.*

**Lowe Alpine, Broomfield, CO**
Web site: lowealpine.com
*Packs, clothing, mountaineering gear, travel gear.*

**Marmot Mountain Ltd., Santa Rosa, CA**
Phone: 707-544-4590
Web site: marmot.com
*Packs, tents, sleeping bags, clothing, gloves.*

**Mountain Safety Reseach/ MSR Inc., Seattle, WA**
Phone: 800-531-9531
Web site: msrcorp.com
*Tents, cooking gear, preserved foods, water-purification gear.*

**Mountainsmith, Golden, CO**
Phone: 800-551-5889
Web site:
  mountainsmith.com
*Packs and sleeping bags.*

**The North Face Inc., San Leandro, CA**
Phone: 800-447-2333
Web site: thenorthface.com
*Packs, tents, sleeping bags, clothing, footwear, travel gear.*

**Outdoor Products, Los Angeles, CA**
Phone: 800-438-3353
Web site:
  outdoorproducts.com
*Packs, sleeping pads, travel gear.*

**Sierra Designs, Emeryville, CA**
Phone: 800-635-0461
Web site: sierradesigns.com
*Tents, sleeping bags, clothing.*

**Wenzel Camping Gear, Everett, WA**
Phone: 877-848-7617
Web site:
  camping-n-gear.com
*Packs, tents, sleeping bags, propane stoves.*

**Woolrich Inc., Woolrich, PA**
Phone: 800-966-5372
Web site: woolrich.com
*Clothing, footwear, travel gear.*

# MAJOR ONLINE RETAILERS
## FOR HIKING GEAR OF ALL KINDS

**Backcountrystore.com**
Phone: 800-409-4502
Web site:
   backcountrystore.com
*Newsletters.*

**L. L. Bean Co.**
Phone: 800-221-4221
Web site: llbean.com
*Catalog; four retail stores
and "factory" stores in seven
states.*

**Bob Ward's**
Phone: 800-800-5083
Web site: bobwards.com
*No catalog; five retail stores
in Montana.*

**Cabela's**
Phone: 800-237-4444
Web site: cabelas.com
*Catalog; eight retail stores
in six states.*

**Campmor**
Phone: 888-226-7667
Web site: campmor.com
*Catalog; one retail store in
New Jersey.*

**Eastern Mountain Sports**
Phone: 888-463-6367
Web site: ems.com
*Catalog; retail stores in 16
states.*

**Outdoor Outlet**
Phone: 800-726-8106
Web site:
   outdooroutlet.com
*Catalog; one retail store in
Utah.*

**Paragon Sports**
Phone: 800-961-3030
Web site:
   paragonsports.com
*No catalog; one retail store
in New York City.*

**REI**
Phone: 800-426-4840
Web site: rei.com
*Catalog; 63 retail stores
in 24 states.*

**Uncle Dan's**
Phone: 888-2GO-HIKE
Web site: udans.com
*No catalog; three retail
stores in Chicago area.*

*Italicized* page references indicate illustrations.

# ABOUT THE AUTHOR

Michael Robbins is a long-time writer and editor in the fields of science and nature. He was the editor-in-chief of *Audubon* from 1991 through 1997 and previously served as an editor of *Museum News, Oceans Magazine,* and *Connection.* He is the author of *Brooklyn: A State of Mind, Birds: A Family Field Guide,* and *High Country Trail: Along the Continental Divide* and coauthor of the children's book *Woodswalk.* His work has been featured in many National Geographic publications, popular travel magazines, and *New York, Rolling Stone, Reader's Digest, Savvy,* and *Popular Science.* Currently, Robbins is, among other pursuits, editorial director of Verandah Media, Inc. (a partnership specializing in magazine consulting, electronic media projects, and book packaging); a partner in the publications firm Palitz + Robbins; contributing editor to *Mother Jones* magazine; and consulting editor to *Discover* magazine.

Also in Storey's *Quiet Sports* series:
**The Kayak Companion,** by Joe Glickman. Expert guidance
for enjoying the paddling experience in water of all types from
one of America's premier kayakers. ISBN 1-58017-485-X.